SNOWFLAKES 2

Even More UNIQUE PAPER SNOWFLAKE PATTERNS *with* STEP-BY-STEP INSTRUCTIONS

JAMIE GOBLE BROCCO

PLAIN SIGHT PUBLISHING • AN IMPRINT OF CEDAR FORT, INC.
SPRINGVILLE, UTAH

Dedicated to my parents who encouraged/tolerated my many childhood projects.

—Jamie

ISBN 13: 978-1-4621-4477-8
ebook ISBN 13: 978-1-4621-4478-5

Published by Plain Sight Publishing, an imprint of Cedar Fort, Inc.
2373 W. 700 S., Suite 100, Springville, UT 84663
Distributed by Cedar Fort, Inc., www.cedarfort.com

Cover and page design and layout by Shawnda T. Craig

Printed in the United States of America

10 9 8 7 6 5 4 3 2 1

Printed on acid-free paper

Contents

PATTERN PAGES AND TEMPLATES

ABOUT THE AUTHOR

Snowflake Basics

ALL SNOWFLAKES ARE UNIQUE

PATTERNS ARE PROVIDED AS A LEARNING TOOL: My hope is that you will gain the confidence to create your own designs!

Be prepared to expand the skills developed in *Christmas Snowflakes 1*.

Don't be afraid to go off-pattern! The snowflakes below are all interpretations of the Candlelight Snowflake Pattern found on the Box Folding Template on page 79.

See QR Code below for the Exaggerated Borders Demo.

SCAN TO VIEW:
Exaggerated Borders Demo

"There is beauty in both simple and complex designs. Find your unique voice!" —Jamie

Snowflake Basics

SUPPLIES & CREATING A SQUARE

SUPPLIES: Paper, Hole Punches: 1/4" (standard) and 1/8", Scissors

OPTIONAL SUPPLIES: Pencil, Paper Clips, or Staples

Experiment with different weights of paper. Newspaper is an ideal weight and texture for beginners. Beware of slick finishes that can cause unnecessary frustration.

The hole punch and scissors must be capable of cutting through twelve layers of paper at once, without hurting your hands or tearing the paper.

Paper clips and staples are optional, but highly recommended for stabilizing paper while cutting and for holding a pattern on top of a folded square of paper.

CREATING A SQUARE: A square piece of paper can be made from a rectangular piece by lining up one side of the paper with the adjacent side, creating a point (45° angle) [See image below].

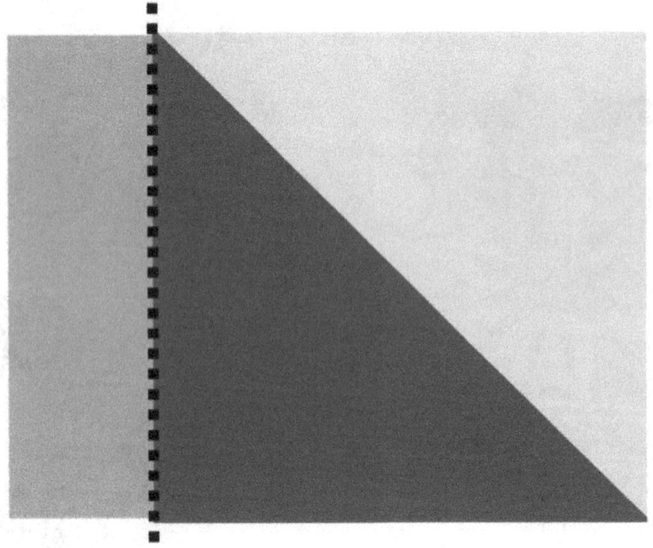

Cut off the excess as shown on the dotted line.

The size of square needed is noted under the bottom point of each pattern. Large snowflakes can be made from squares of wrapping paper or newspaper.

DO THE SCISSORS REALLY MATTER?

Left: A well-used pair of school scissors was used for this snowflake. The cutting seemed to be going well, but the unfolding was frustrating—all those little teeth kept catching on each other!

Some scissors will not have the strength to go through twelve layers of paper, while some scissors may need to be sharpened. Other scissors may have a lot of chips from years of use that make them too frustrating to use. Other things to keep in mind are whether the tips of the scissors are blunt or sharp. [See comparison below].

Right: Four layers of cardstock showing cuts made by three different pairs of scissors. The first cut was made by small sharp tip scissors and the other two cuts were made by blunt tip scissors. If cuts are made all the way to the tip of the scissors, the blunt tipped scissors leave a cross cut. The central pair of scissors left a significant tear!

Experiment with the scissors that you plan to use, so you will know their capabilities. Each has strengths and you can switch back and forth between them.

As the designs become more intricate, the type and sharpness of scissors used makes a difference in the ease of completing designs.

TIP: A small pair of sharp tipped scissors works well in tight spaces such as inside letters. Scalpels or hobby knives may also be used, but they are not child friendly.

Snowflake Basics

PAPER TYPES

> **WARNING:** Snowflake obsession may involve trying to create snowflakes from all kinds of paper! The recycle bin is a good place to look for inspiration [See *Christmas Snowflakes 1* for more reviews].

Coffee filter

COFFEE FILTERS (left): Are a favorite of beginners. The circle shape eliminates the ears and makes folding into thirds much easier. Not all filters are manufactured the same. When using a hole punch, there are often hanging scraps. But coffee filters are sturdy and cut well with scissors. Filters are fun for adding tie-dye effects as they are easily dyed with food coloring or by using water soluble markers and spraying with water. They make excellent skirts for paper dolls [See QR Code on facing page].

MAGAZINES (bottom left): Often have bright colors and fun graphics which can add or detract from the snowflake design. Unfortunately, the pages are often slick, which can be frustrating. Staples can help stabilize your work. Some magazine pages are too thick to retain details and can be difficult to cut through twelve layers at once.

ORIGAMI PAPER (bottom center): Comes in squares, and handles folds and cuts well. It comes in a wide variety of colors and patterns. Sometimes the center of the paper is white and shows through as you are cutting. The scissors can sometimes rub off areas of color as you go around curves.

GARDEN CATALOGS (bottom right): Have a wide variety of colors and textures in photographs, which can add or detract from the snowflake design. The quality of the paper varies widely from being newspaper or magazine-like.

Magazine

Origami paper
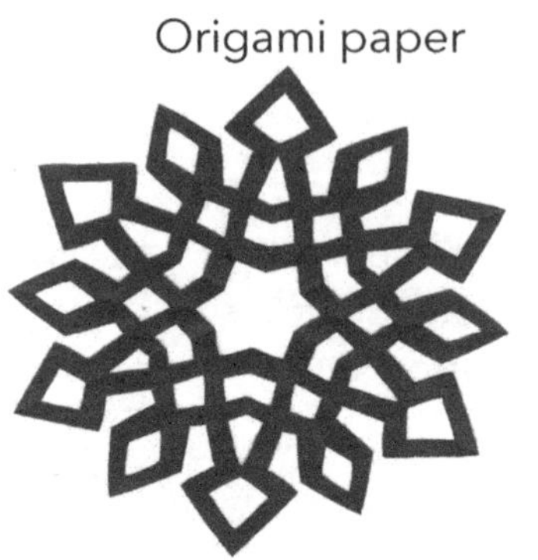

Garden catalog

Napkin

Napkin

SNOWFLAKE BASICS

NAPKINS (above): Napkins tend to be thin. They often tear when cut and don't punch cleanly, leaving hanging scraps. They sometimes cut more cleanly when four snowflakes (forty-eight layers) are cut at once. Texture and patterns can be an asset or a distraction. Often, irregularities in color and texture can occur. Unfolding can be frustrating as the napkins tend to catch on themselves and tear easily.

Construction paper

CONSTRUCTION PAPER (left): Is thick but airy. It feels like the scissors are gumming through the folded paper. The thickness of the folds causes distortion and loss of detail.

*Note: The pattern for the 5" snowflake on this page can be found on page 90.

SCAN TO VIEW:
Paper Dolls: Ballerinas

SCAN TO VIEW:
Paper Comparisons

Snowflake Basics

FOLDING

CONCISE FOLDING DIRECTIONS

1. Fold the square in half diagonally.
2. Fold the resulting triangle in half by bringing the small points together.
3. Steps 3 and 4: Fold the remaining triangle into three parts creating a 30° angle at the bottom and "ears" at the top.

After folding, the "ears" can be left on. [See page 15, or removed, see page 73.]

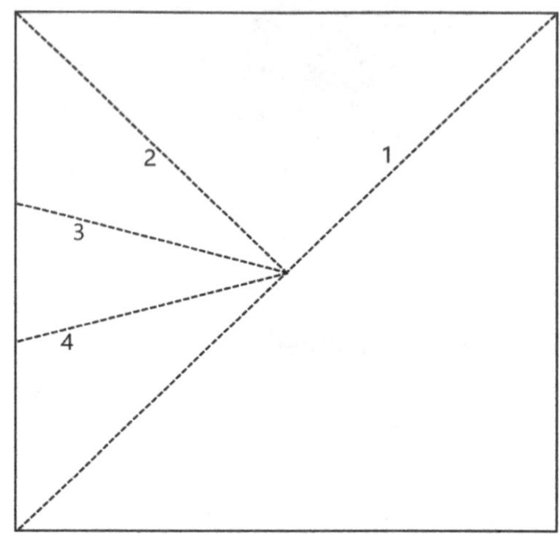

EXPANDED FOLDING DIRECTIONS

The shading of the Box Folding Template [See page 78] shows the 30° angles which will be created in the center of the square. The expanded directions include the number 1 for reference. Keep the last step, number 4, down while folding to avoid covering up the directions.

1. Fold the square in half diagonally.

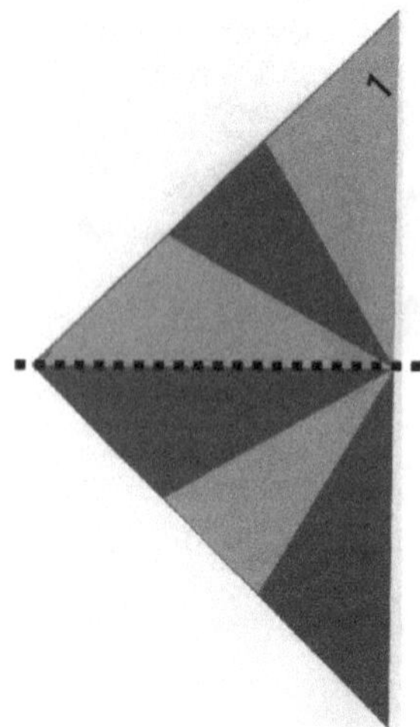

2. Fold the resulting triangle in half by bringing the small points together.

3 and 4: Fold the triangle into three parts, creating a 30° angle at the bottom and "ears" at the top.

*Note: Since numbers 3 and 4 are facing down, these folds may seem backwards at first.

SNOWFLAKE BASICS

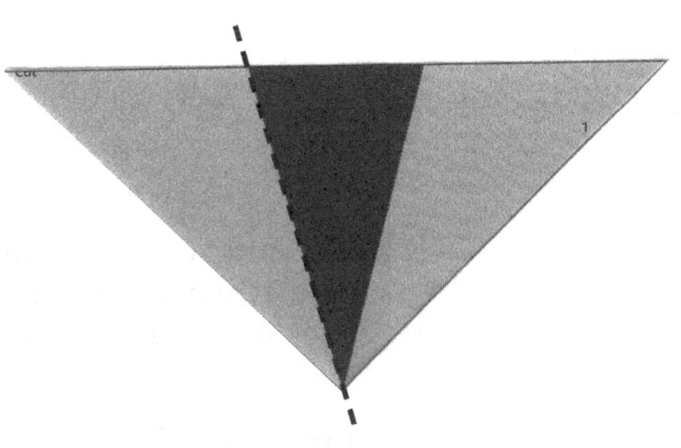

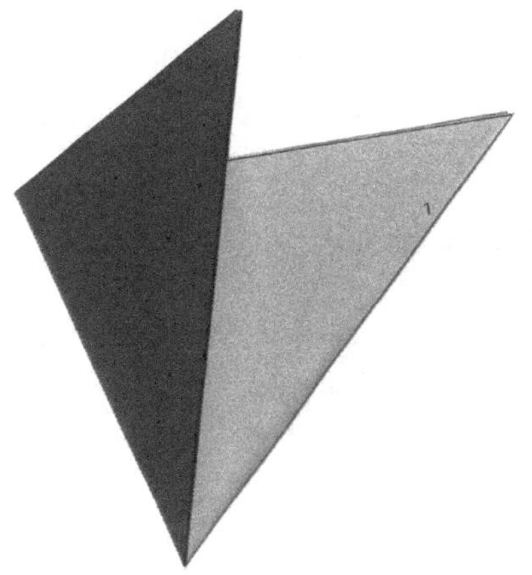

3. With number 3 facing down, fold up along line 3 to begin dividing the triangle into three parts.

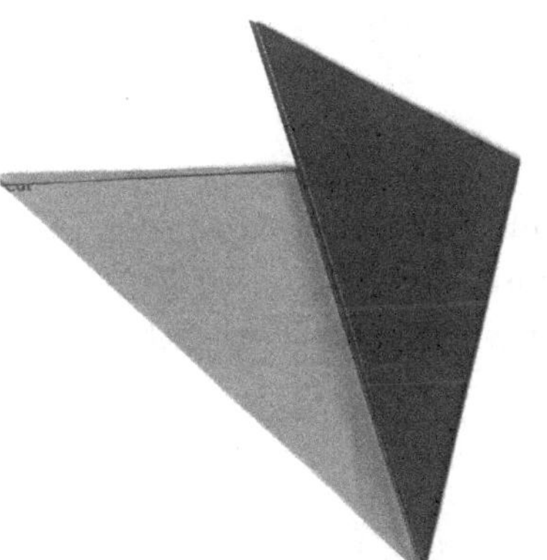

4. Unfold 3. With number 4 facing down, fold up along line 4.

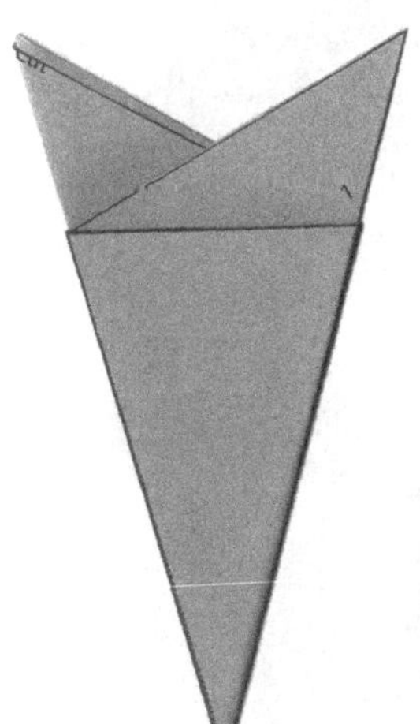

Refold 3: The looser edge (two folds instead of one) will be tucked into the center. This is especially beneficial when using slick paper, to prevent sliding. Crease fold 3 again to accommodate the four additional layers of paper.

SCAN TO VIEW: YouTube Video showing how to fold the Box Folding Template on page 78

SCAN TO VIEW: YouTube Video showing how to fold a circular piece of paper or a Coffee Filter

Snowflake Basics

THE EARS

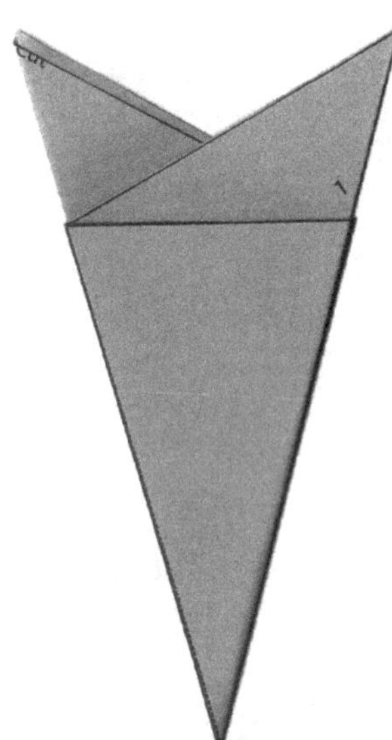

ONCE THE SQUARE OF PAPER IS FOLDED, there will be "ears" sticking up above the main triangle. Be careful not to extend your snowflake design onto these "ears."

One side of the folded square has an edge which acts as the cut-off point [See illustrations on the left and in the bottom left corner]. The illustration below shows what the paper looks like with the ears removed.

The folded square, without its "ears", is the base of all the snowflakes.

WHEN SHOULD I REMOVE THE "EARS?" That's up to you! Some people prefer to remove them immediately, but the "ears" can come in handy for holding the pattern to the folded paper with paper clips, etc.

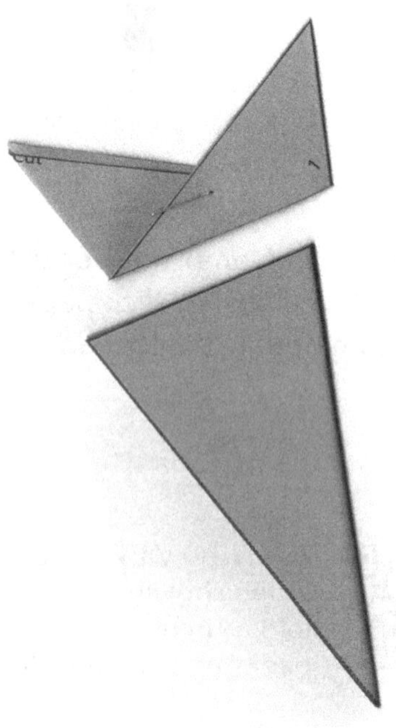

Snowflake Basics

PATTERN ON TRIANGLE X 12

Right: The pattern on the triangle is repeated twelve times in the snowflake. [See pattern on page 90].

Below: The pattern for the Love Snowflake gives you an idea of the alternating mirror images that occur due to the folding of the paper. The word 'Love' within the snowflake is repeated twelve times. If the Love Snowflake is displayed in a window, 6 of the repetitions will be easily read from either side [See Love Snowflake Directions on page 11].

Snowflake Basics

DESIGN

IN DESIGN, you must consider the stability of the finished snowflake. Some snowflakes are beautiful, but the design is difficult to unfold successfully. For others, the connections are not stable enough to prevent twisting or distortion of the finished snowflake. Generally speaking, it is best to leave at least two folds, or connections, on both of the long sides of the triangle to provide stability when unfolded.

WORDS

Whether spoken, sung, or written, our primary way of expressing gratitude is through words. The repetitive and mirrored nature of snowflakes means, when displayed in a window, half of the words can be read from outside and half from inside, showing our gratitude to anyone who sees.

In deciding what paper to cut away and what to keep, you must first consider the word that you want to write: Do the letters extend below the line? How will the word touch the folds? Generally speaking, you will want the word to touch both of the folds on each of the long sides of the triangle at least twice for stability. To accomplish this, consider the writing lines shown on the facing page. The letters don't need to perfectly follow the lines, nor do the lines need to be parallel or equidistant, but the letters must touch each other!*

The style of letters used is a personal preference. Commonly students will write their name in cursive and then cut a border around the letters. Use a highlighter or shading on the pencil lines to create cutting lines. Try bubble letters, calligraphy, all capital letters, printed text . . . remember, the letters must touch each other!*

Facing Page, Top: The word 'Love' does not have any letters extending below the line, so it is written using the long side of the triangle as the bottom line [See page 11].

Facing Page, Middle: Joy breaks the "rules" by not following the writing lines exactly, to allow for a fancy J, and using the lower part of the y as a long fold on one side instead of preserving two folds on each side [See *Christmas Snowflakes Book 1*].

Facing Page, bottom: The word 'Rejoice' is written in all caps in a perspective style where the letters get smaller the closer they are to the center. [See Rejoice Snowflake on page 85].

WHAT INSPIRES YOU?

Share your inspiration and designs with #ChristmasSnowflakes

*Alternatively, letters can be cut away rather than kept: creating a stencil-like snowflake with paper left around the letters and connections made to the interior of the letters [See Stencil-like Nativity on pages 67 and 85].

Snowflake Basics

USING PATTERNS

THE PAPER FOLDING TECHNIQUE [seen on page 6] creates a triangle (below the ears) which is the base of all the snowflakes. Most of the patterns [starting on page 76] are designed for triangles created by folding 8.5" squares of paper. The size of the beginning square for each pattern is noted beneath it.

You can use the patterns in this book in several ways:

1. Cut out a pattern from the pattern pages and place it on top of a folded paper. Then cut through the pattern and folded paper at the same time. Paper clips or staples may be used to hold the pattern in place. Examples are shown throughout this book.
2. Use the pattern as a stencil by cutting away the shaded portion and tracing the design onto the folded paper [See example below]. This works well with patterns already used in option 1.
3. Sketch the design, or parts of complex designs, onto the folded paper with a pencil.
4. Use the patterns for inspiration and as a rough guide. Some people are able to cut snow-flakes freehand simply by looking at the patterns.

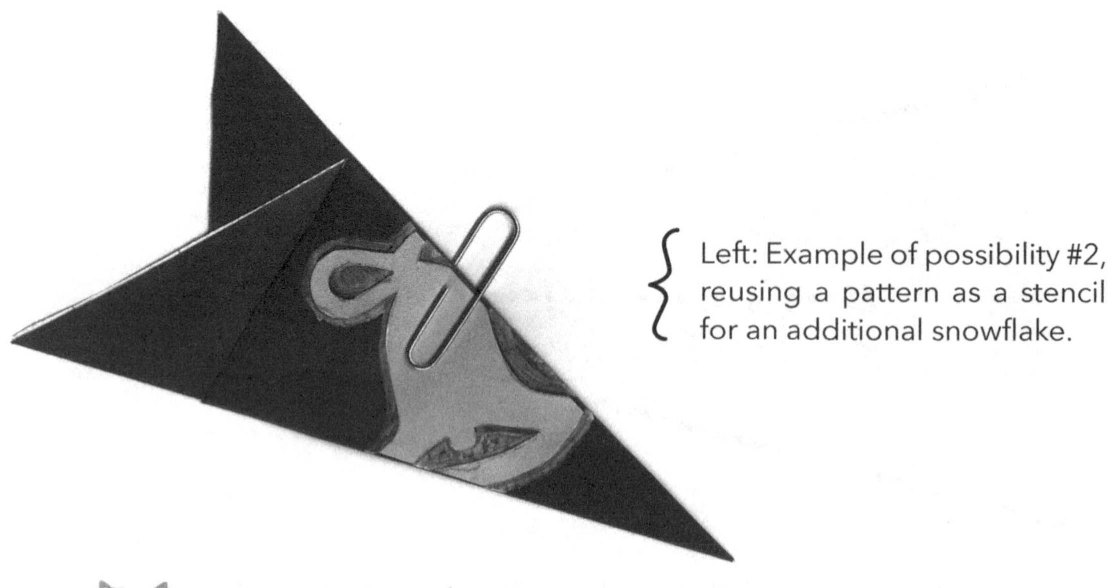

Left: Example of possibility #2, reusing a pattern as a stencil for an additional snowflake.

TIP: Make copies of the patterns, so you can keep the book intact. Copies can be made for personal use.

TIPS: The shaded areas of the patterns are meant to be cut away.

- The word fold is used to mark a folded area that needs to be left intact.
- If there are two snowflakes in the same pattern, the word divide is used to show the division between the two snowflakes.
- Remember to unfold snowflakes carefully!

WHEN CUTTING AWAY THE SHADED AREAS of the pattern, leave the shaded area above the pattern intact for paper clips or staples to stabilize the pattern. Then start working toward the center of the snowflake by cutting away the shaded areas from the outer edges inward (the center acts as a stabilizing point).

EXCEPTIONS TO WORKING FROM THE OUTSIDE IN:

Use the hole punch first if needed

If there is an area of the pattern that is more intricate or which the rest of the pattern revolves around start there. This gives you more wiggle room to make changes as needed. For example, if you are making a heart snowflake, work on the hearts first to make sure they are to your liking [See below right].

Staples: For beginners (especially those focusing on scissor skills), it is helpful to use multiple staples for stability (make sure to staple in areas that will be cut away). The stapled areas will be the last to be cut away [See center below].

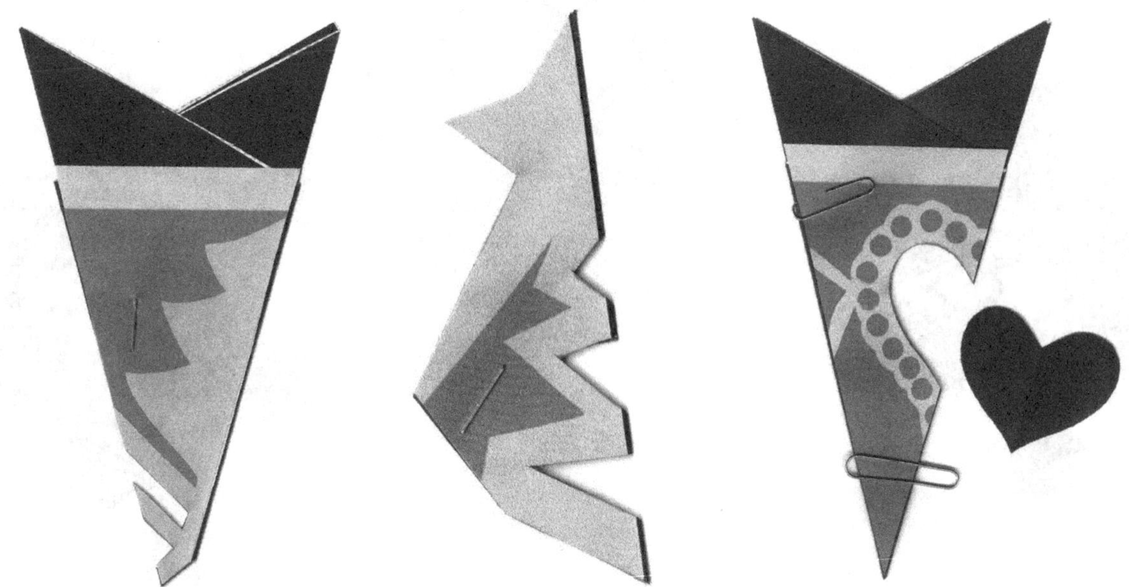

Above: Cut the shaded areas of the patterns away, and read the above descriptions for more details.

Cutting Snowflakes

EVERGREEN TREES, SNOWMEN, AND SHOOTING STARS

IN EACH PATTERN, the shaded areas are meant to be cut away with scissors or a hole punch. When cutting snowflakes, the most important thing is to leave part of the fold on both of the long sides of the triangle. The more complex the design, the more attention needs to be paid to the folds. Folded areas (to be left intact) are marked on each snowflake with the word fold.

The word divide in the Shooting Stars Snowflake Pattern indicates the division between two snowflakes. Some patterns are two-in-one! After cutting out a snowflake, any pieces leftover with at least part of both folds intact can be used to make an additional snowflake.

Folding and cutting are both essential to the success of the snowflake. The more intricate the pattern, the more important it is to have a well folded piece of paper with tightly creased folds. Each pattern has a number at the bottom point indicating the size of the starting square of paper.

Shown with a standard size punch, the eyes and buttons of the snowmen below can be made with a variety of sizes and shapes.

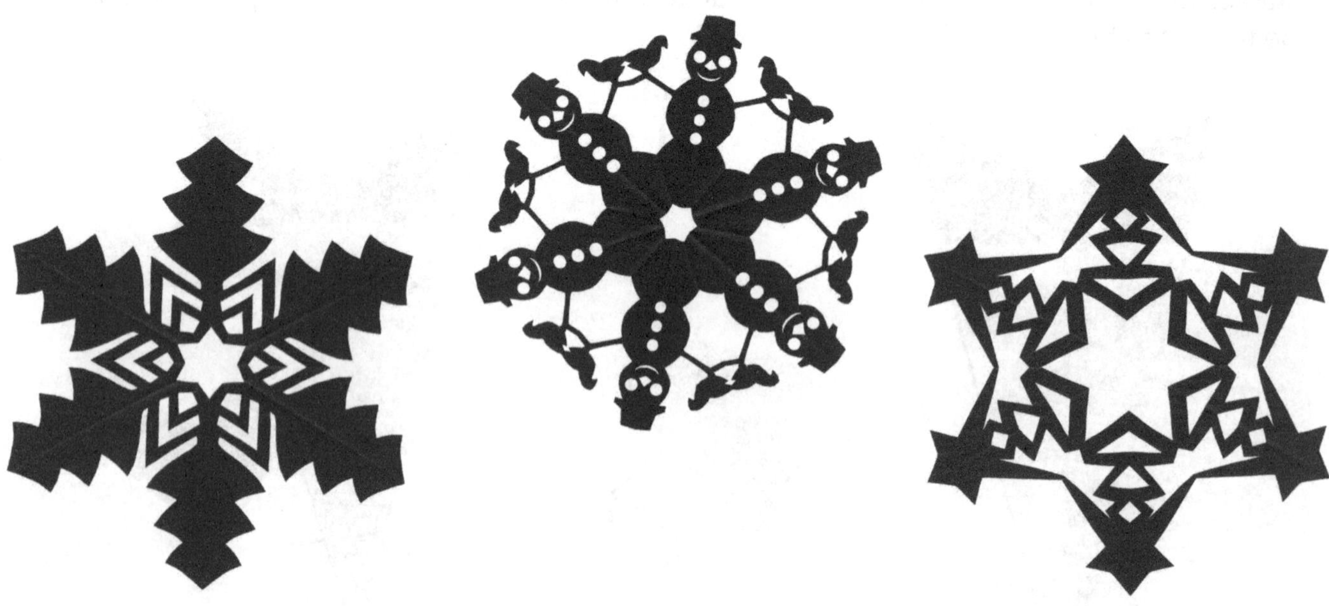

TIP: When cutting, pause at the points and corners to turn the paper before continuing on with the scissors.

EVERGREEN TREES

*See pattern on page 80.

THE EVERGREEN TREES SNOWFLAKE is a good example of a snowflake that perfectly follows the suggestion to remove the shaded areas from the outside in. Follow along with the steps and images below.

Step 1: Attach pattern to the folded paper.

Steps 2–4: Leaving the outer edge intact for stability (that is where the staple is located), begin cutting away the shaded areas from the outside in [See images labeled Steps 2, 3, 4 below].

Step 5: Remove the outside edge of the snowflake.

Step 6: Unfold and admire your finished snowflake.

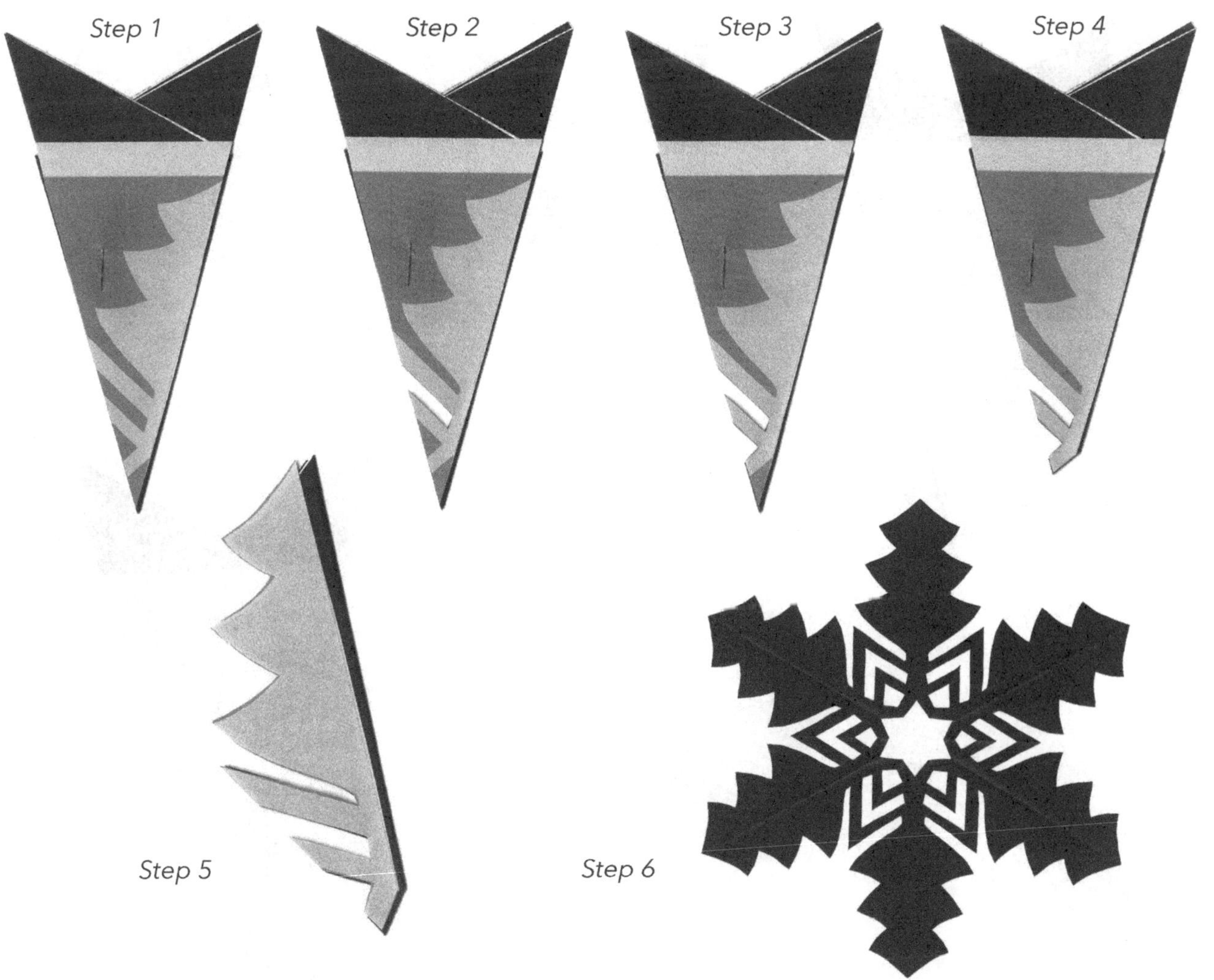

SNOWMEN WITH DOVES

**See pattern on page 80.*

Follow along with the steps and their corresponding images below.

Step 1: Attach pattern to folded paper.

Step 2: Use hole punch to punch out the eye and buttons.

Step 3: Add the other details to the face–changing personality, if desired.

Steps 4 & 5: Start cutting out the dove. If you choose, you can make this task easier by breaking it into parts, or challenge your scissor skills and try to cut out the area under the dove's tail in one piece. Remember to pause at the points as you are cutting to turn the paper.

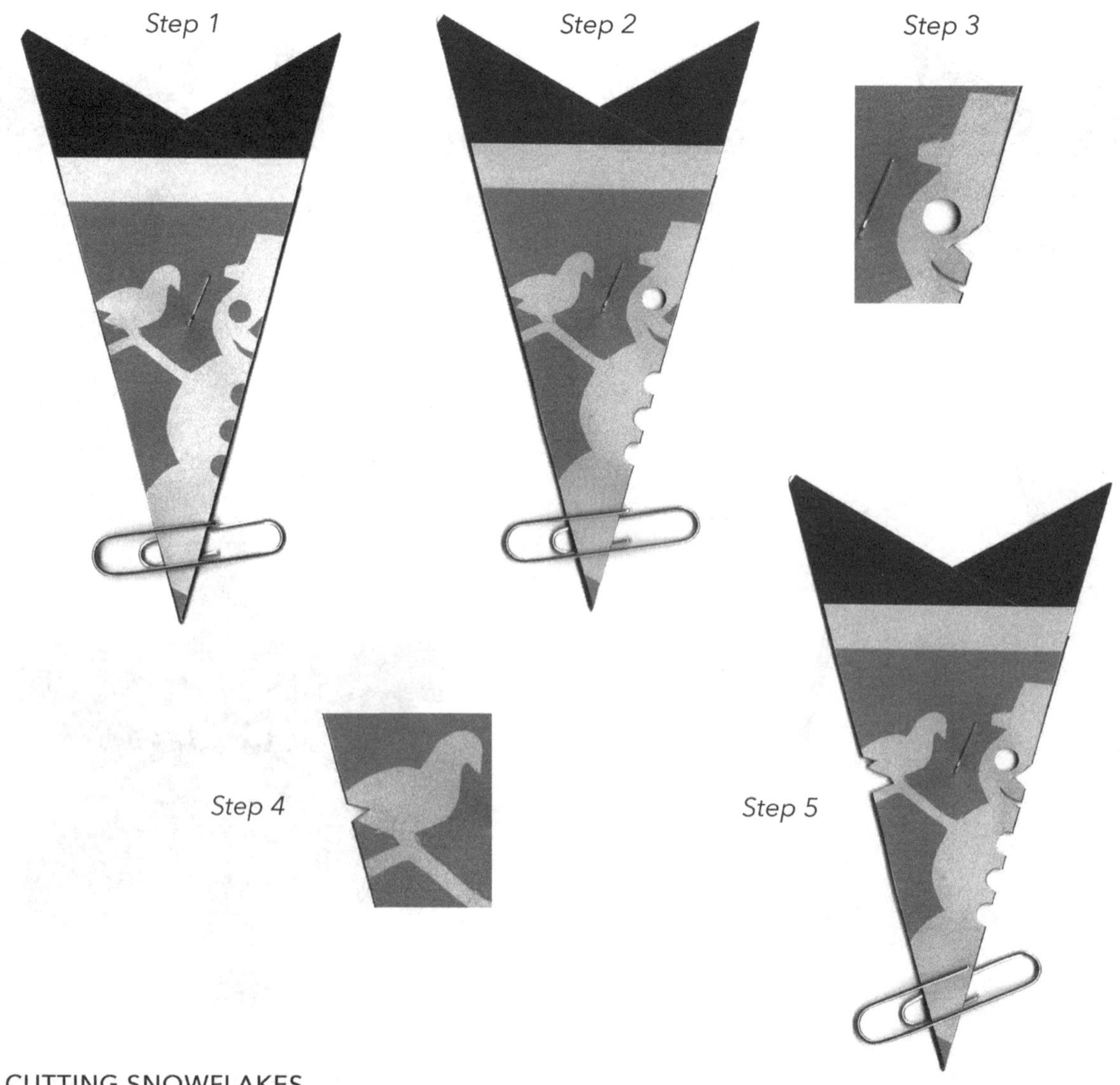

Step 6: Cut away the shaded area next to the snowman's body.

Step 7: Cut out the center.

Step 8 & 9: The dove's neck is a bit tricky, so remove the outer edge in multiple pieces if needed. Small scissors are helpful for tight turns.

Step 10: Unfold and enjoy

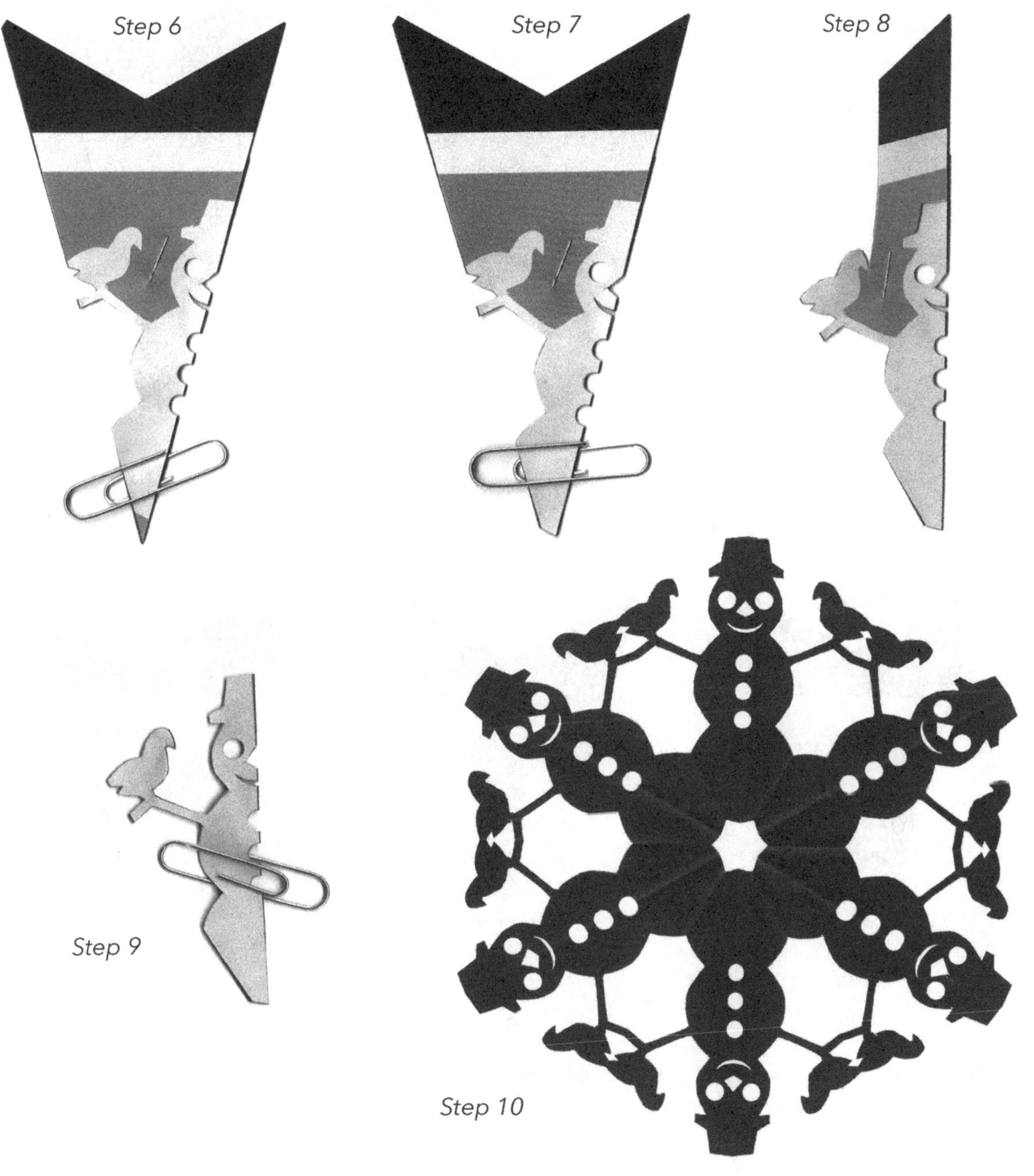

SHOOTING STARS

**See pattern on page 80.*

Follow along with the steps and their corresponding images below.

Steps 1-3: Attach pattern to the folded paper and start removing the shaded areas from the outside in, leaving the outside and stapled areas until the end.

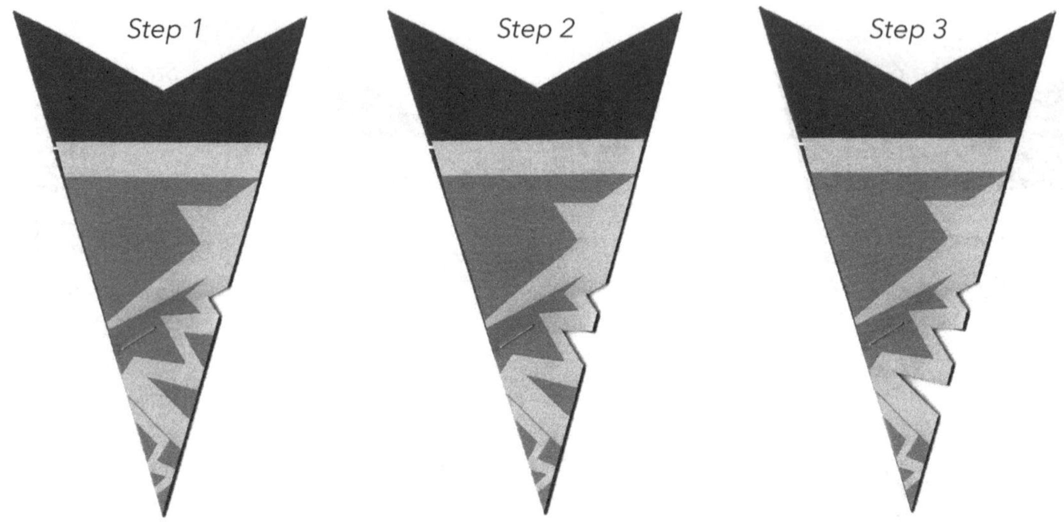

TIP: For ease of handling the smaller snowflake, leave two-in-ones attached until details are finished.

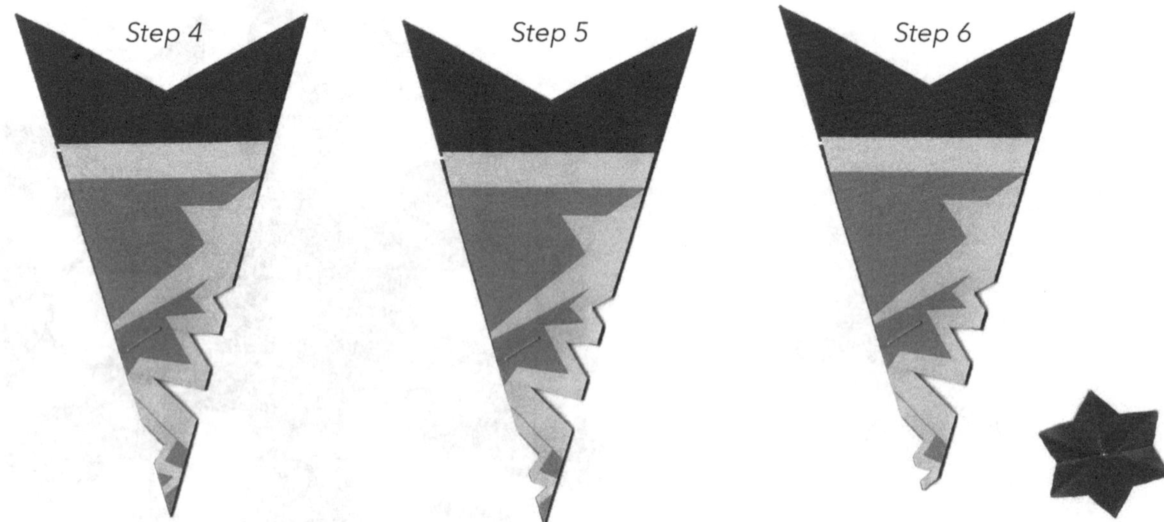

Steps 4-6: Start cutting away the details of the two-in-one (the second smaller pattern), leaving the areas of the divide for later.

Step 7: The divide is a simple line striaght across, but it is easier to remove the shaded area if you make the short cuts before the dividing cut. Start at the bottom of the shaded area and cut toward the dividing line. Then make the division.

Step 7

Unfold and enjoy!

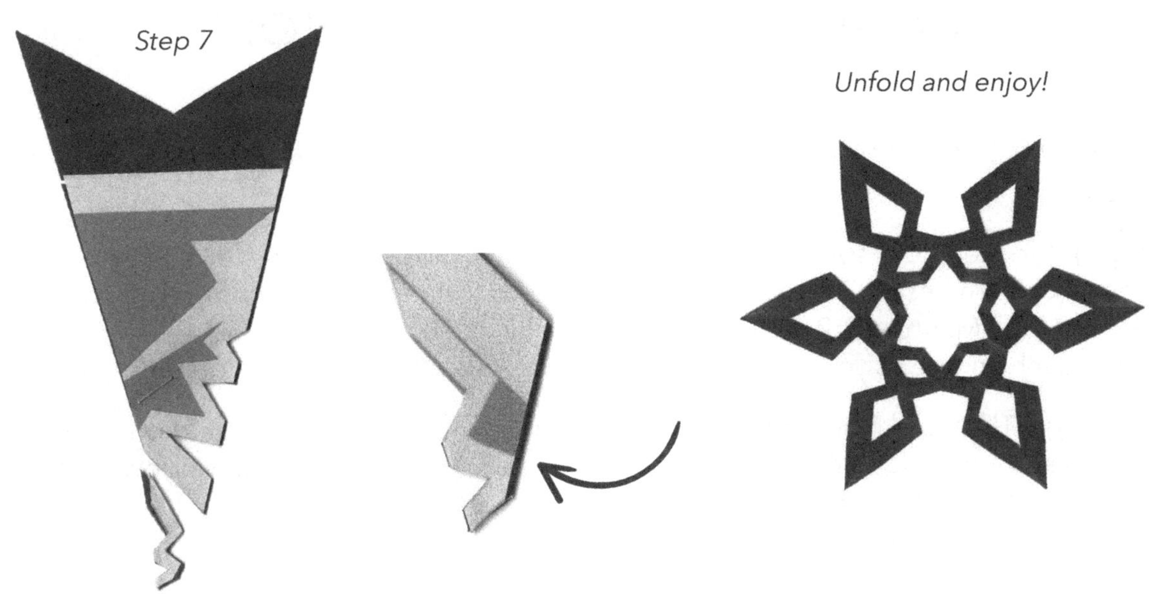

Step 8: Remove the shaded area outside of the snowflake.

Step 9: Cut away the stapled area. Unfold and enjoy!

Step 8

Step 9

Unfold and enjoy!

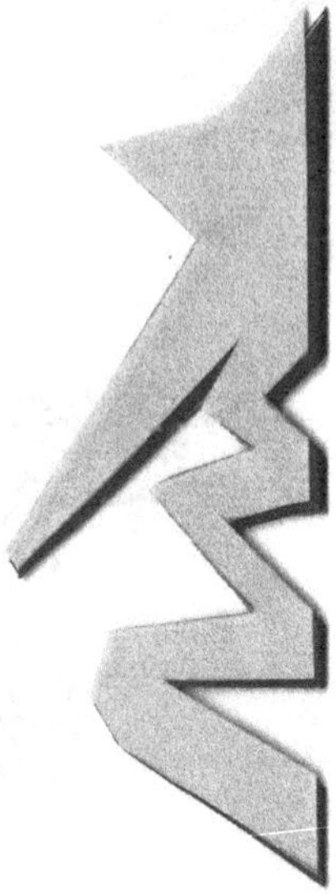

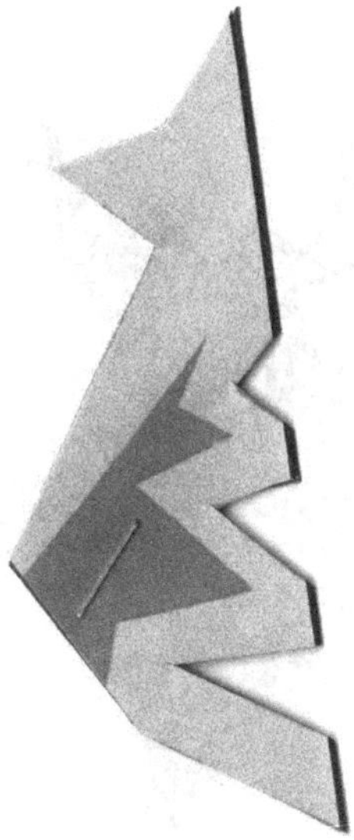

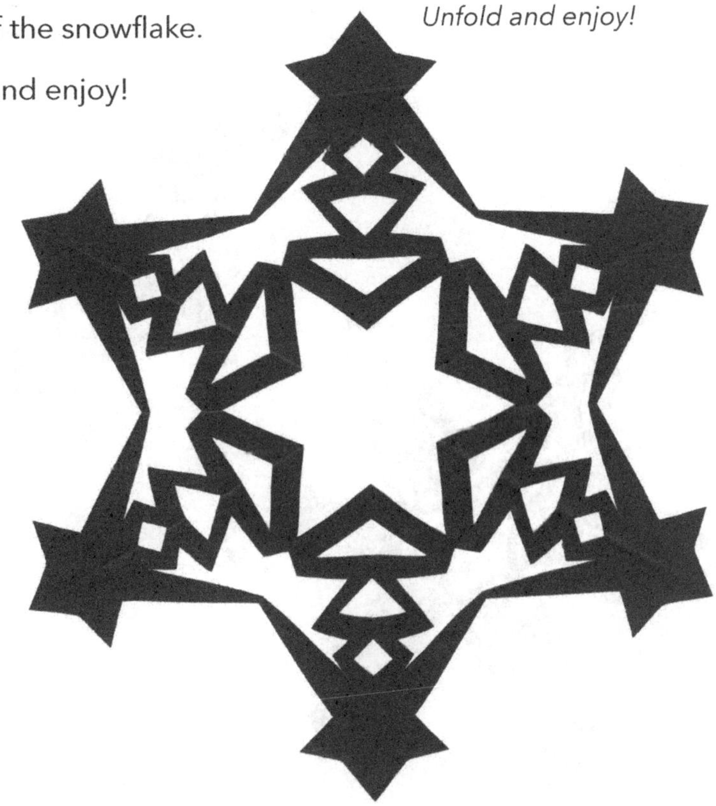

Cutting Snowflakes

RINGING OUT A JOYOUS NOEL

ON CHRISTMAS MORNING, BELLS RING OUT: proclaiming the birth of our Lord and Savior, Jesus Christ!

The top of the steeple displays a diamond which symbolizes the new star that appeared in the heavens when Jesus Christ was born. If desired, the diamond shape may be replaced with a cross [See Matthew 2:2, 3 Nephi 1:19-21, Helaman 14:5 "And behold, there shall a new star arise, such an one as ye never have beheld; and this also shall be a sign unto you"].

Bottom Right: The word Noel can be made as a separate snowflake by cutting on the dashed line [See pattern on page 86]. When word snowflakes are displayed in a window, half of the words can be easily read whether you are indoors or out.

BELL TOWER

*See pattern on page 81.

Follow along with the steps and their corresponding images below.

Step 1: Attach pattern and cut out the half-diamond from the steeple.

Step 2: The small bell is easier to cut out in three parts.

Step 3: Next, cut out the outside of the large bell.

The diamond in the steeple represents the star that shone the night of Christ's Birth, but feel free to alter the pattern to include a cross if you prefer.

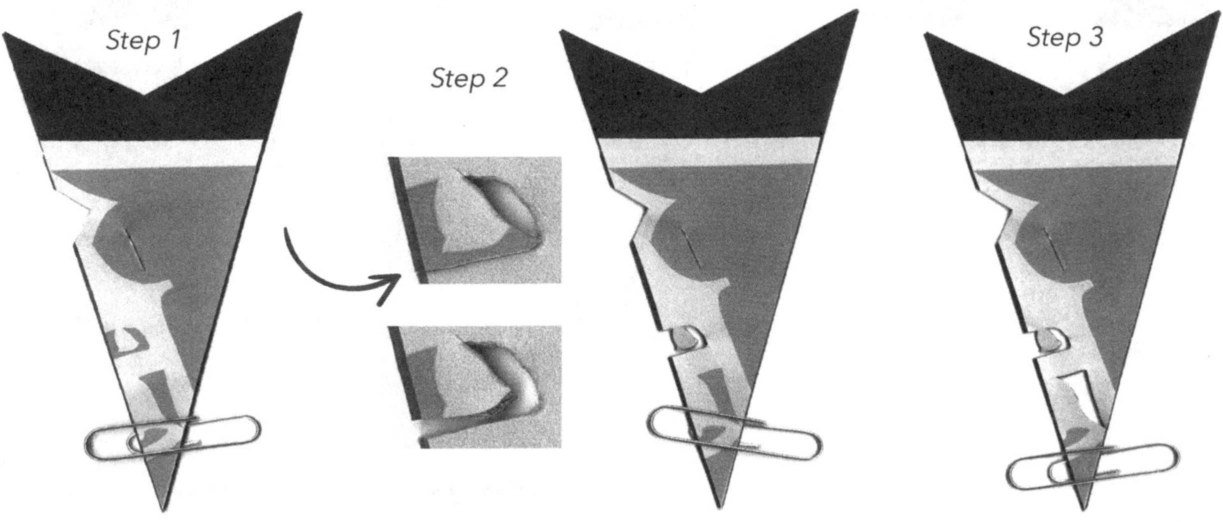

Step 4: Cut out the center of the bell.

Step 5: Cut away the shaded areas in the center and outside of the snowflake. Unfold and admire.

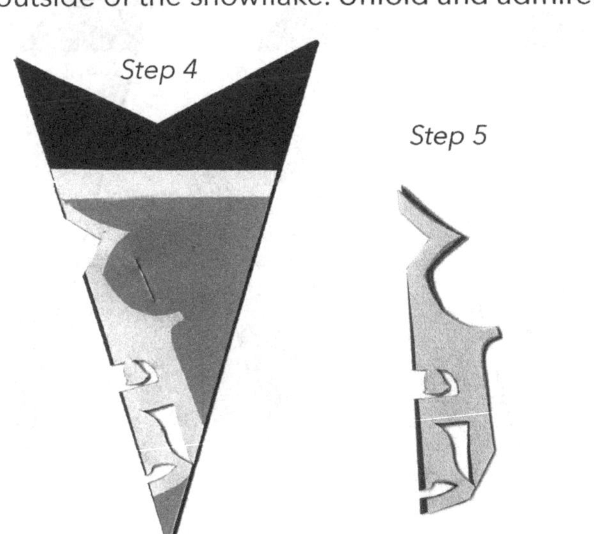

Unfold and enjoy!

HANDBELLS

See pattern on page 81.

Follow along with the steps and their corresponding images below.

Steps 1–5: Attach pattern to folded paper. Use a hole punch to start the opening in the loop. Use a small pair of scissors to finish cutting the tear drop shape. Continue cutting away the shaded areas, working your way toward the center.

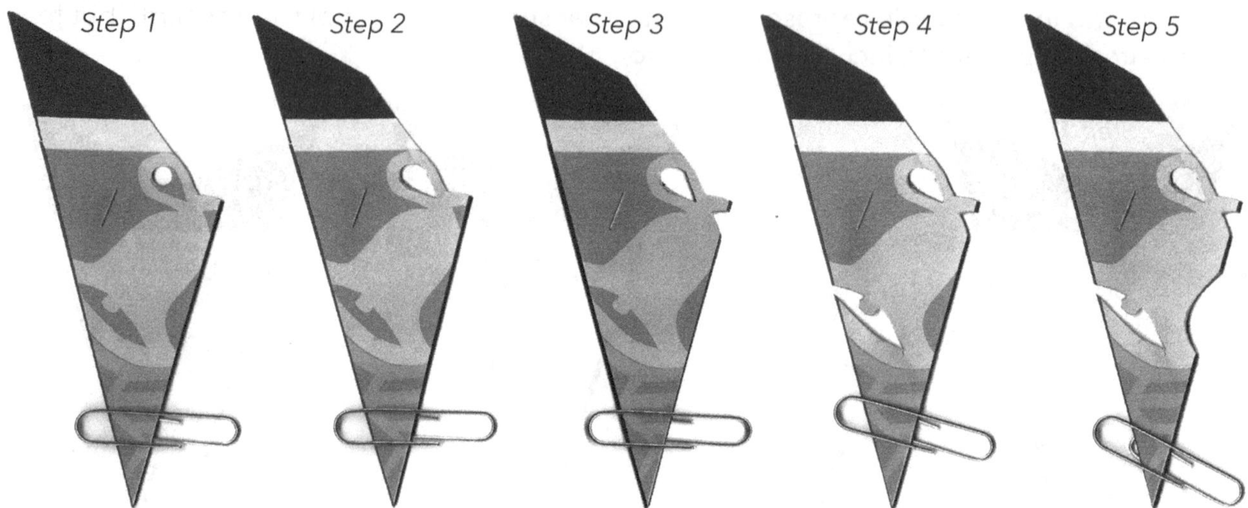

Steps 6–10: Ignore the divide line for now. Continue removing the shaded areas, working your way toward the center.

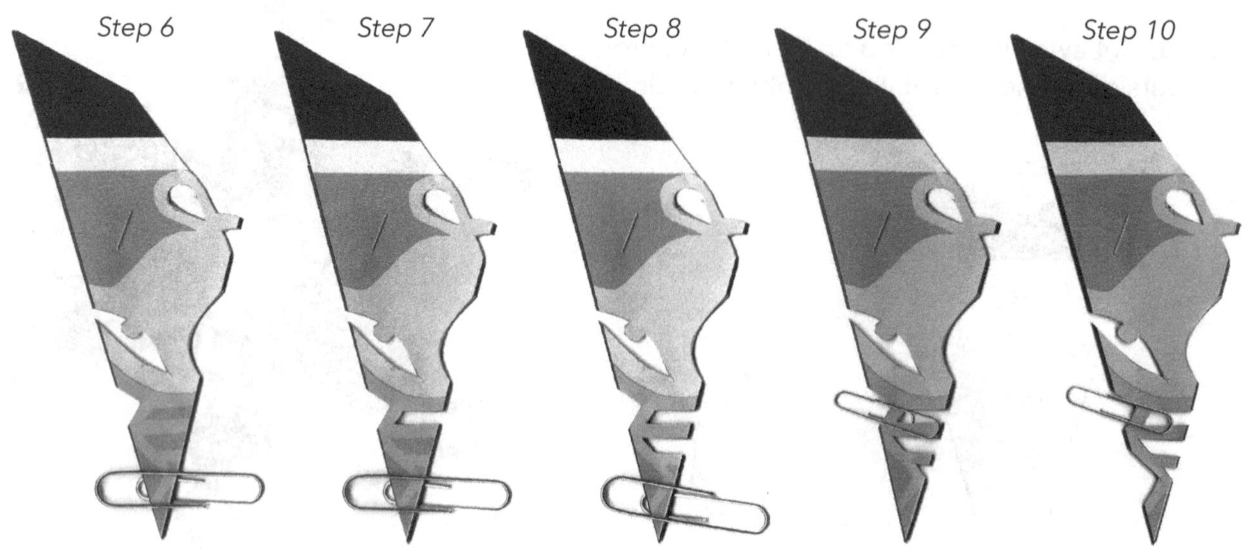

Steps 11–12: Remove center and cut along the divide line.
Unfold and admire the small snowflake.

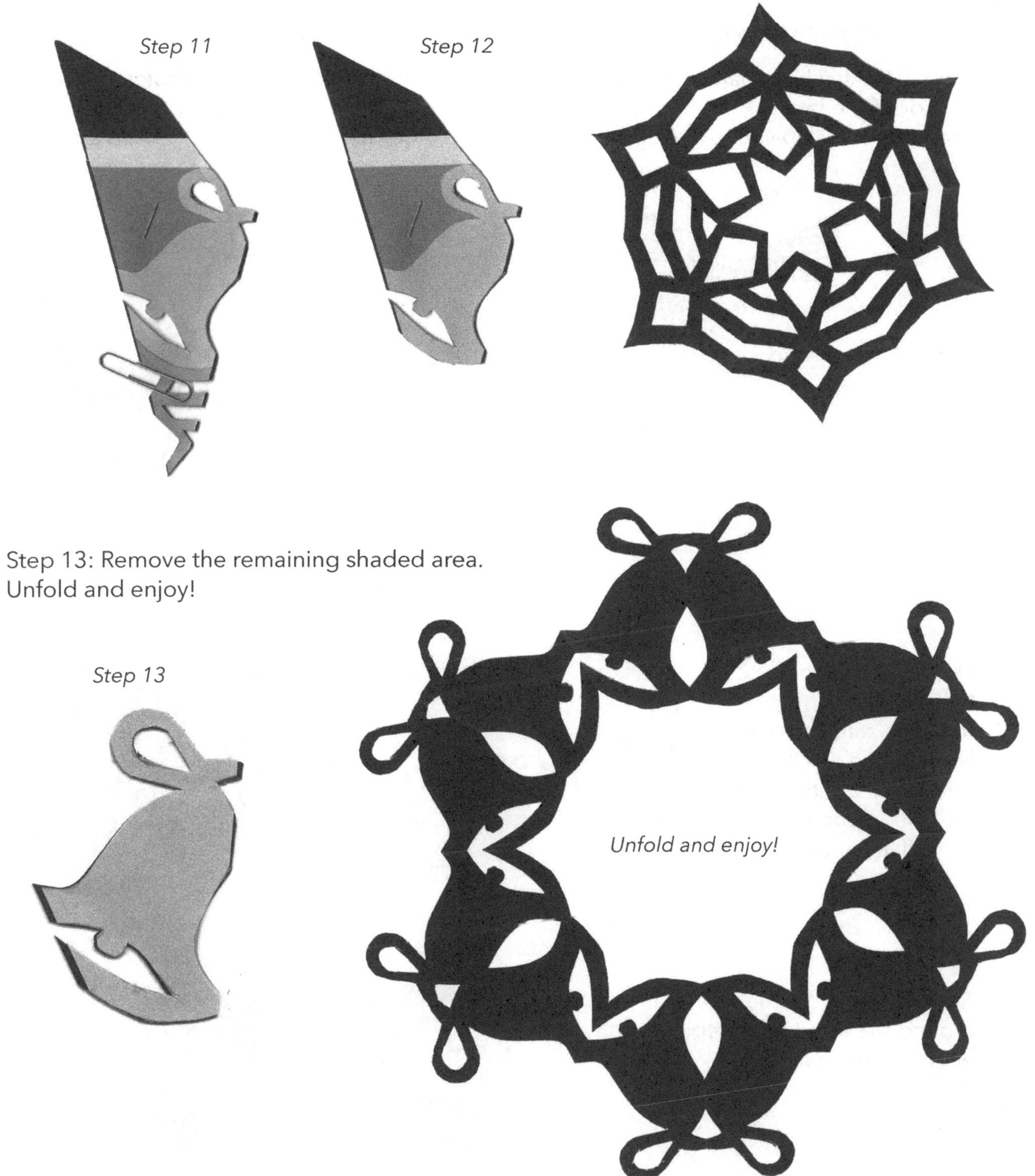

Step 13: Remove the remaining shaded area.
Unfold and enjoy!

BELL TOWER WITH NOEL

*See pattern on page 86.

Follow along with the steps and their corresponding images below.

Steps 1–3: Attach the pattern to the folded paper. Use hole punches to make holes to start the interior of the letters 'o' and 'e.' 'O' has two standard size punches. 'E' has one small punch. Then use a small pair of sharp tipped scissors to carefully finish cutting out the interior of the letters.

Steps 4–7: Cut out the half diamond shape from the steeple. Then work on the small bell, removing a little at a time if needed for a smooth even cut.

Steps 8–9: Cut out the area in and around the large bell, beginning with the area inside.

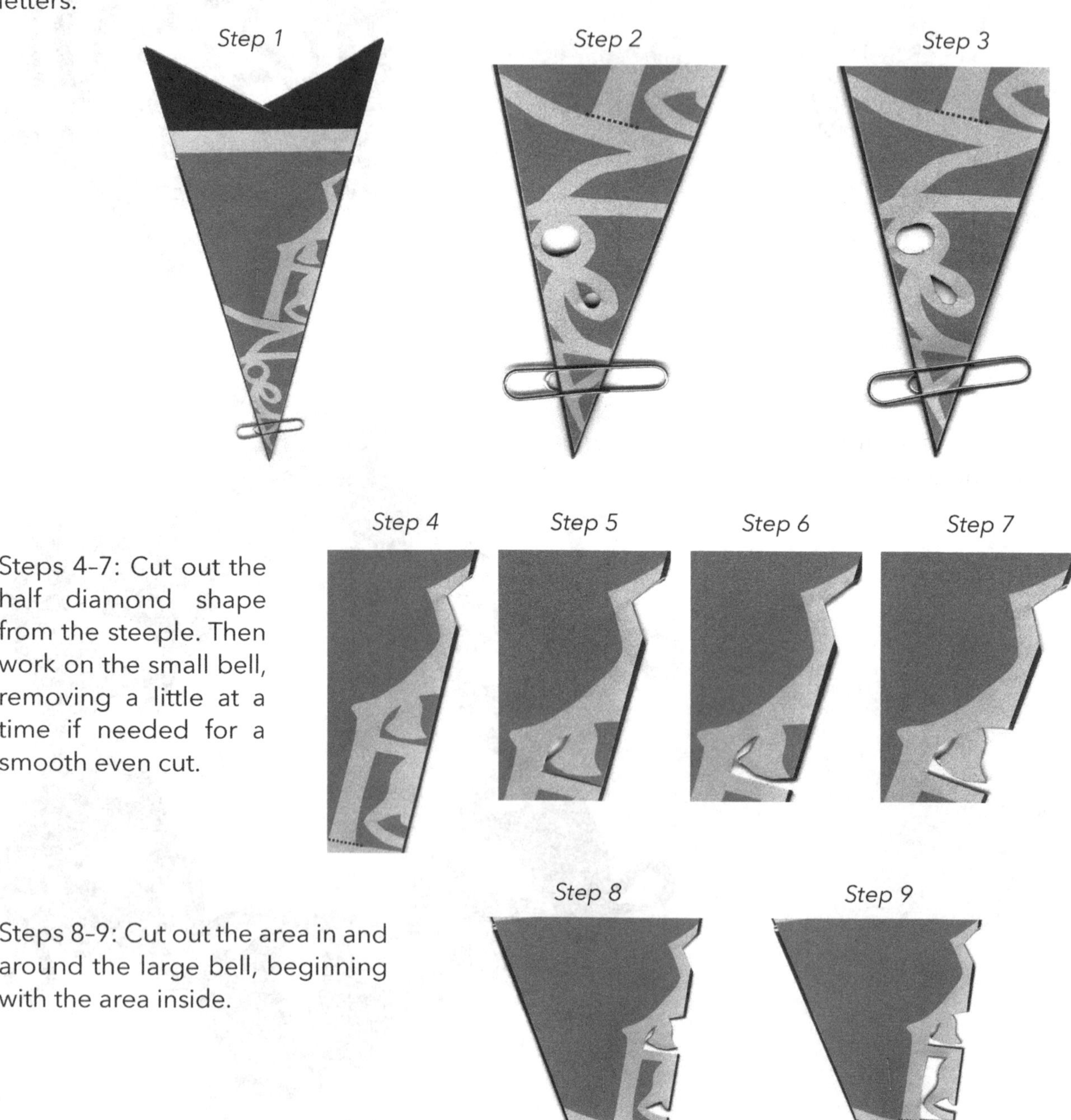

Steps 10–14: Work your way toward the center, removing the shaded areas. Note: in the center above the vowels, the more complicated area was removed in sections.

Step 10 *Step 11* *Step 12* *Step 13* *Step 14*

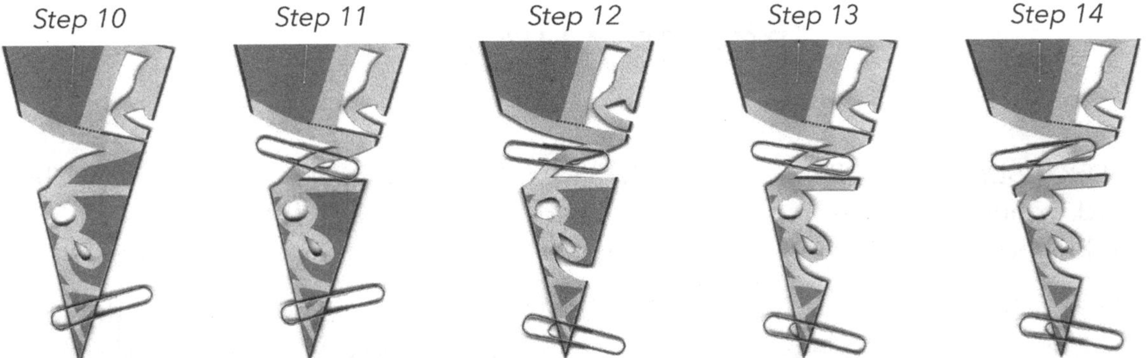

Steps 15–19: Continue removing the shaded areas, working your way toward the center. In the center illustration, the shaded area may appear to be interior space, but it is accessible from the edge of the paper.

Step 15 *Step 16* *Step 17* *Step 18* *Step 19*

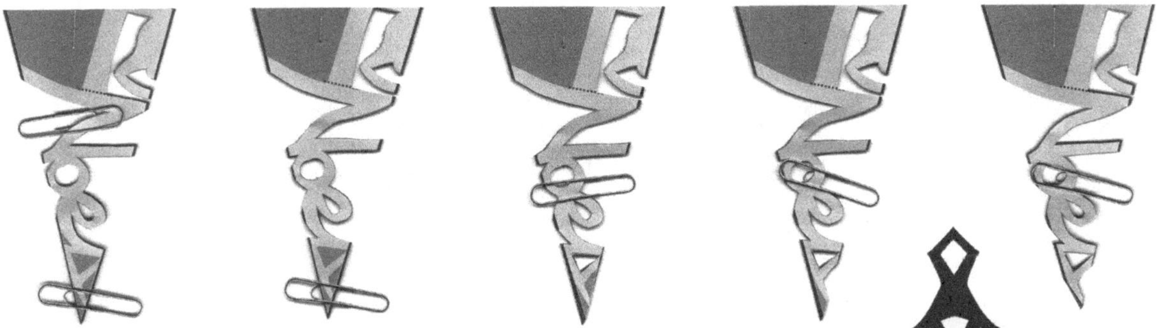

Step 20: Remove the remaining shaded area. Unfold and enjoy!

Step 20

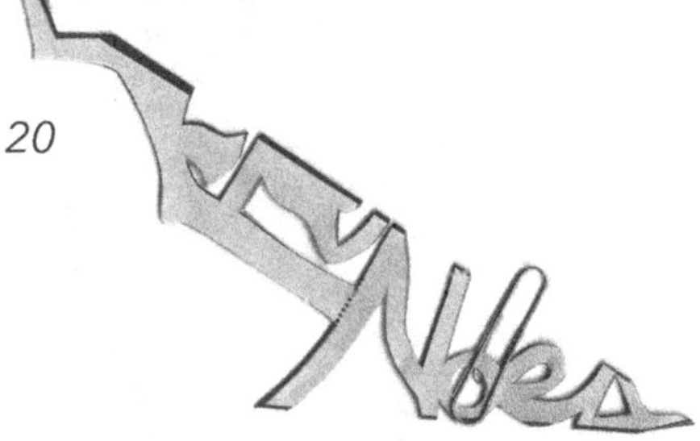

Unfold and enjoy!

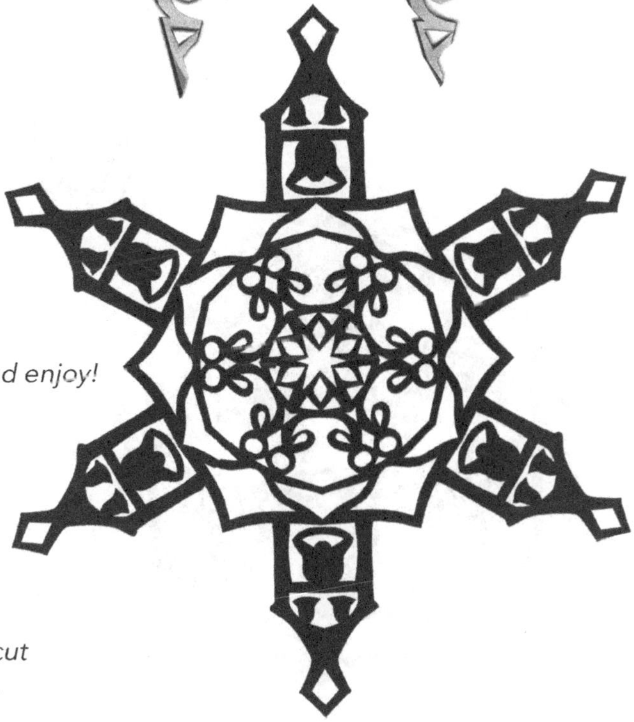

Note: The dashed line on this pattern is an alternative cut line, for those who want to make a word snowflake: Noel.

Cutting Snowflakes

PEACE AND LOVE

WONDROUSLY JOYOUS FEELINGS COME as we think of our Savior, Jesus Christ! They can be hard to put into words, but that doesn't stop us from trying! [See Galatians 5:22, Alma 58:11, Philippians 4:7 and 13 "I can do all things through Christ which strengtheneth me!"]

A hole punch will come in handy for creating words; it creates an opening for the tip of the scissors. Start with the inside of the letters. For the tear shaped openings in the 'L' and 'E's, use the hole punch to create the bulbous end.

The center snowflake, Hearts and Diamonds, provides an opportunity to practice with a hole punch. The inside of the heart is smooth, while the outside appears ruffled with lace as it follows the curves of the punches.

HEARTS AND DIAMONDS

**See pattern on page 81.*

Follow along with the steps and their corresponding images below.

Steps 1–4: Attach the pattern to the folded paper. Make sure you are satisfied with the shape of the heart. Now is the time to make adjustments if you desire. Use a hole punch to create the lacey effect around the heart. Cut out the interior of the diamond. Remove the center of the folded paper. Remember to echo the curves of the hole punches to enhance the lacey effect.

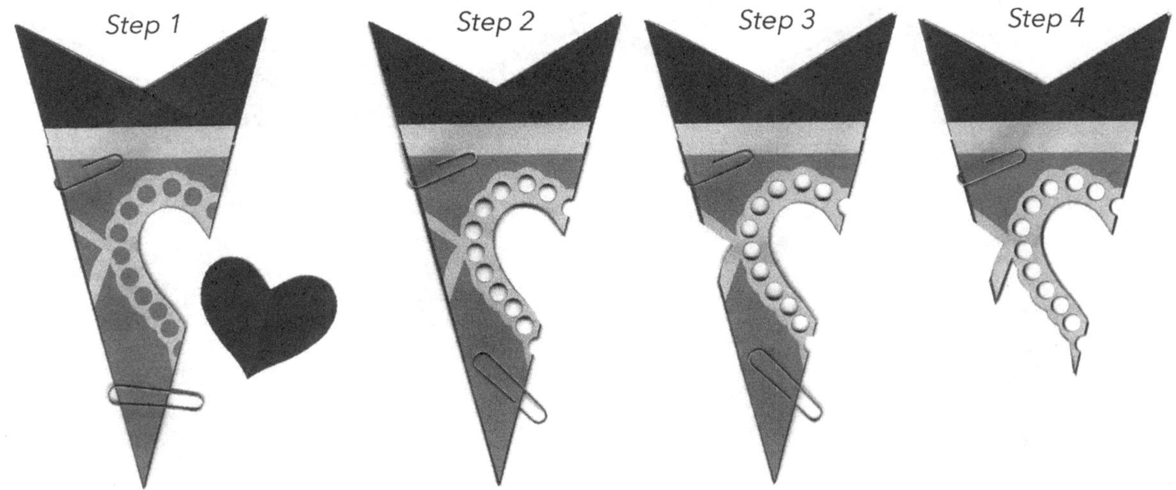

Step 5: Remove the remaining shaded area from the snowflake pattern. Unfold and enjoy! The Interior has great possibilities as a two-in-one!

PEACE

See pattern on page 82.

Follow along with the steps and their corresponding images below.

Steps 1-4: Attach the pattern to the folded paper. Use a hole punch to start the interior of the letters. Use a small pair of sharp tipped scissors to finish cutting out the interior of the letters. Cut out the area under the 'P' and between the 'E' and 'A.' The larger area stabilized with a staple will be cut out later.

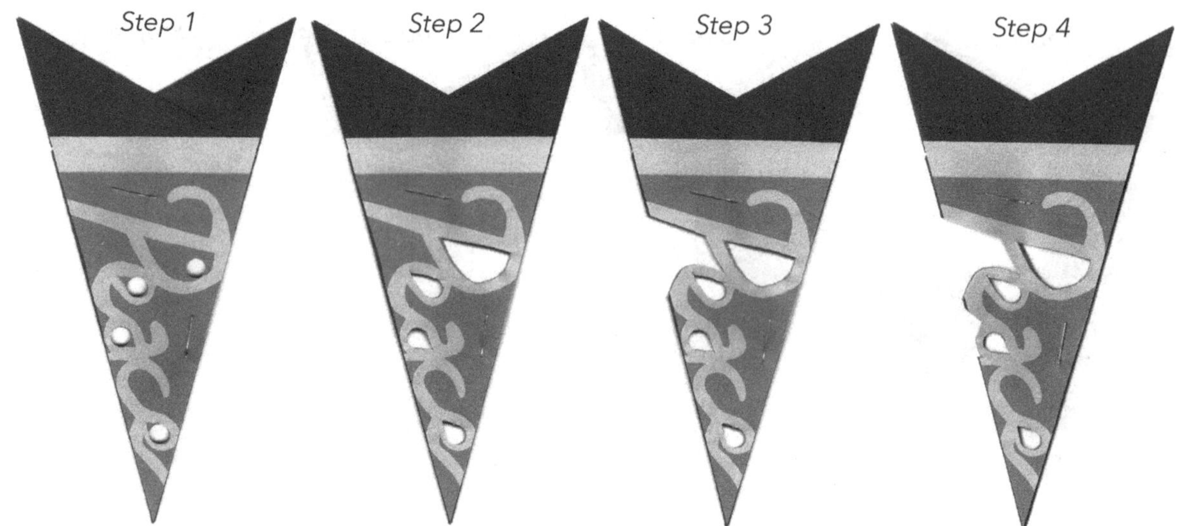

Steps 5-8: Continue cutting away the shaded areas until you reach the center of the folded paper.

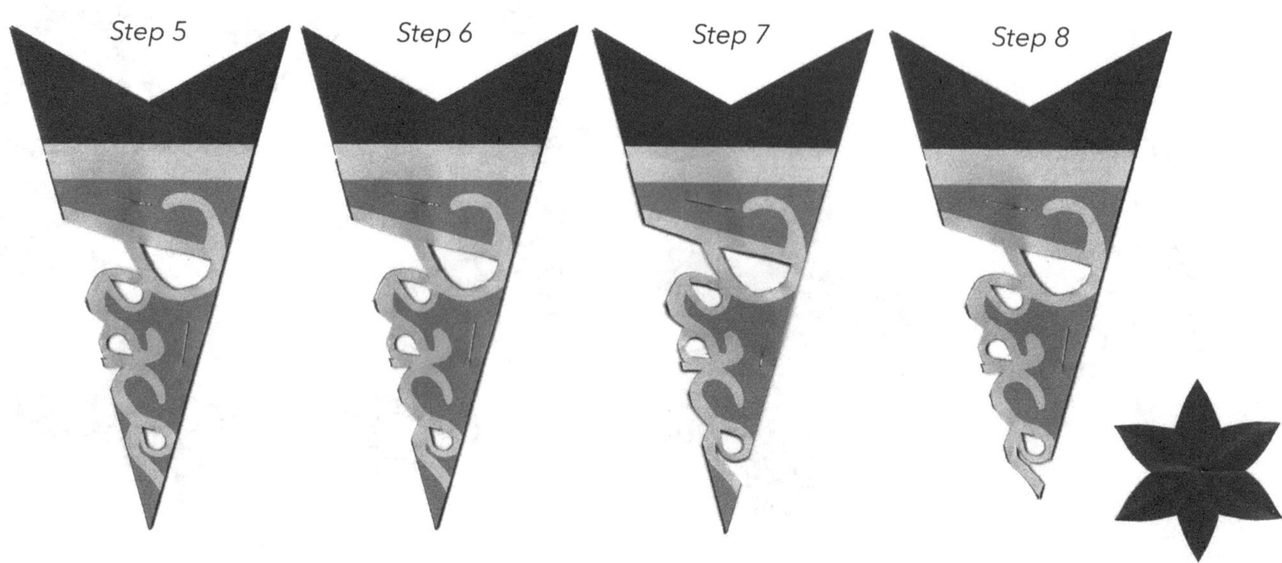

Steps 9–12: Take advantage of the stability of the staple as you cut away the large shaded area, leaving it for last.

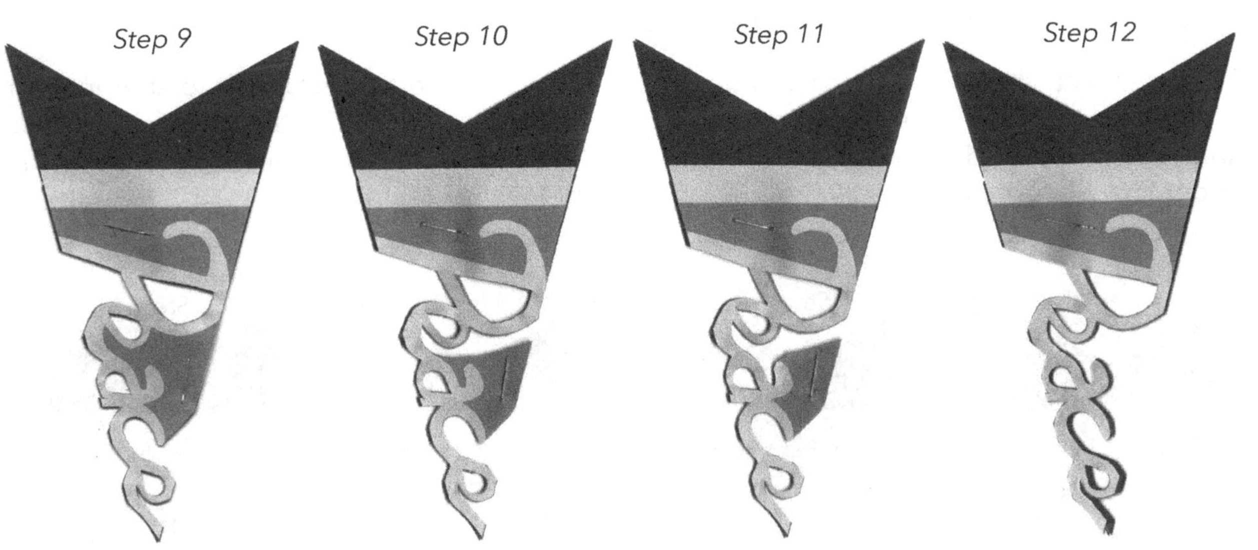

Steps 13–14: Divide the shaded area around the outside of the snowflake to make removal easier. Unfold and enjoy!

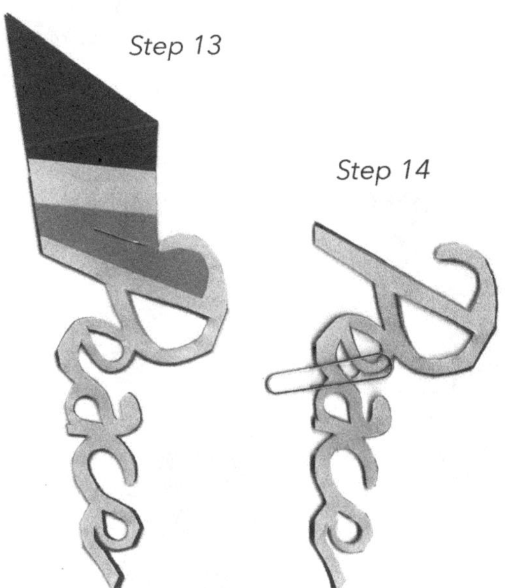

Unfold and enjoy!

LOVE

**See pattern on page 82.*

Follow along with the steps and their corresponding images below.

Steps 1-4: Attach the pattern to a folded piece of paper. Use a hole punch to start interior spaces; use a pair of small sharp tipped scissors to finish the space. For the top of the 'O,' use an access cut [See dotted line on left illustration]. While the staple provides stability for the larger space, start cutting away the shaded areas below the 'L' and 'V.'

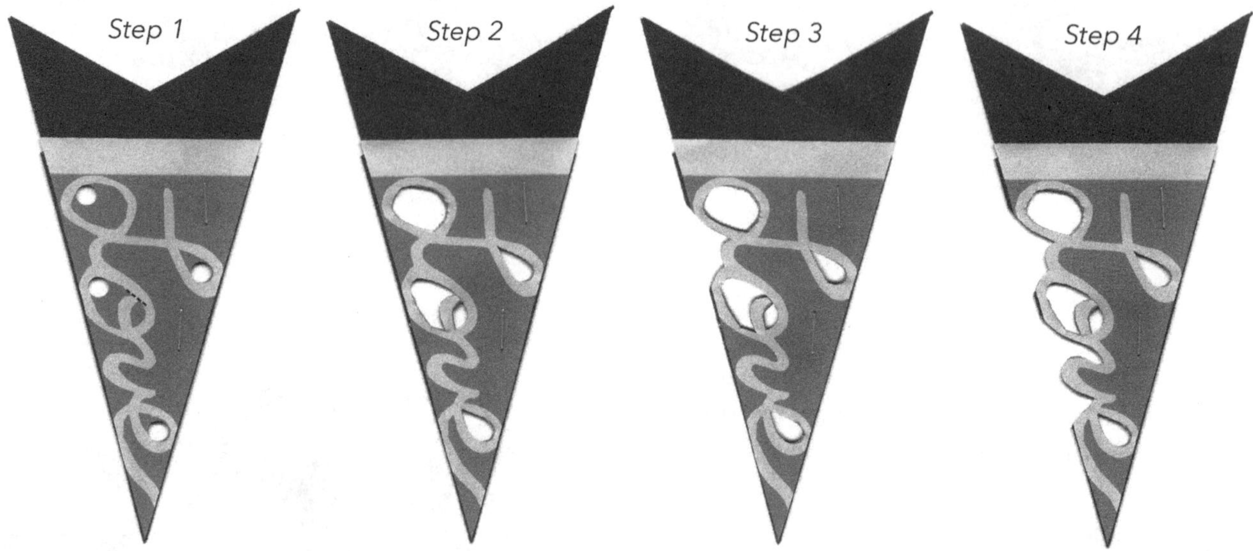

Steps 5-6: Continue cutting away the shaded areas that are not stapled until you reach the center point.

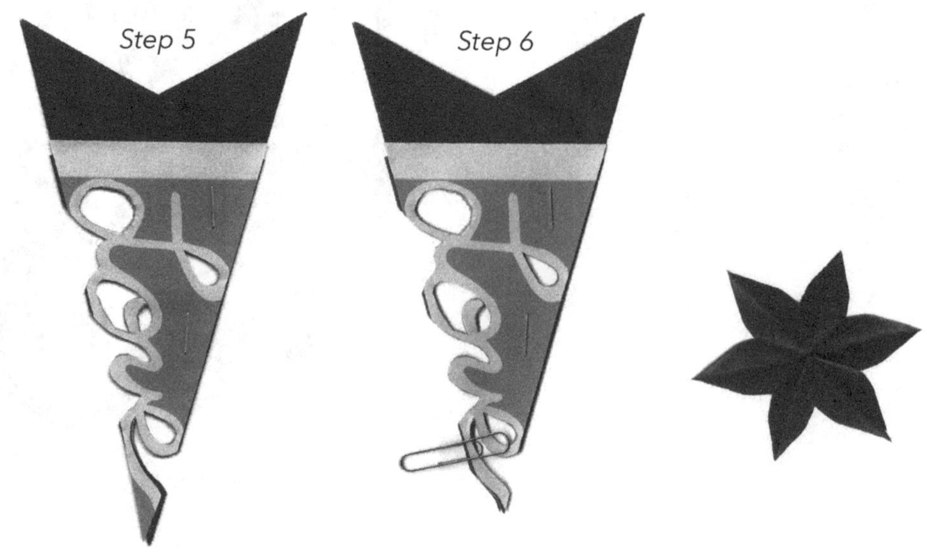

Steps 7–8: Take advantage of the stability of the staple and divide the shaded area into smaller portions if needed for removal.

Step 9: Remove the shaded area from the outer edge of the pattern. Divide into multiple areas if needed. Unfold and enjoy!

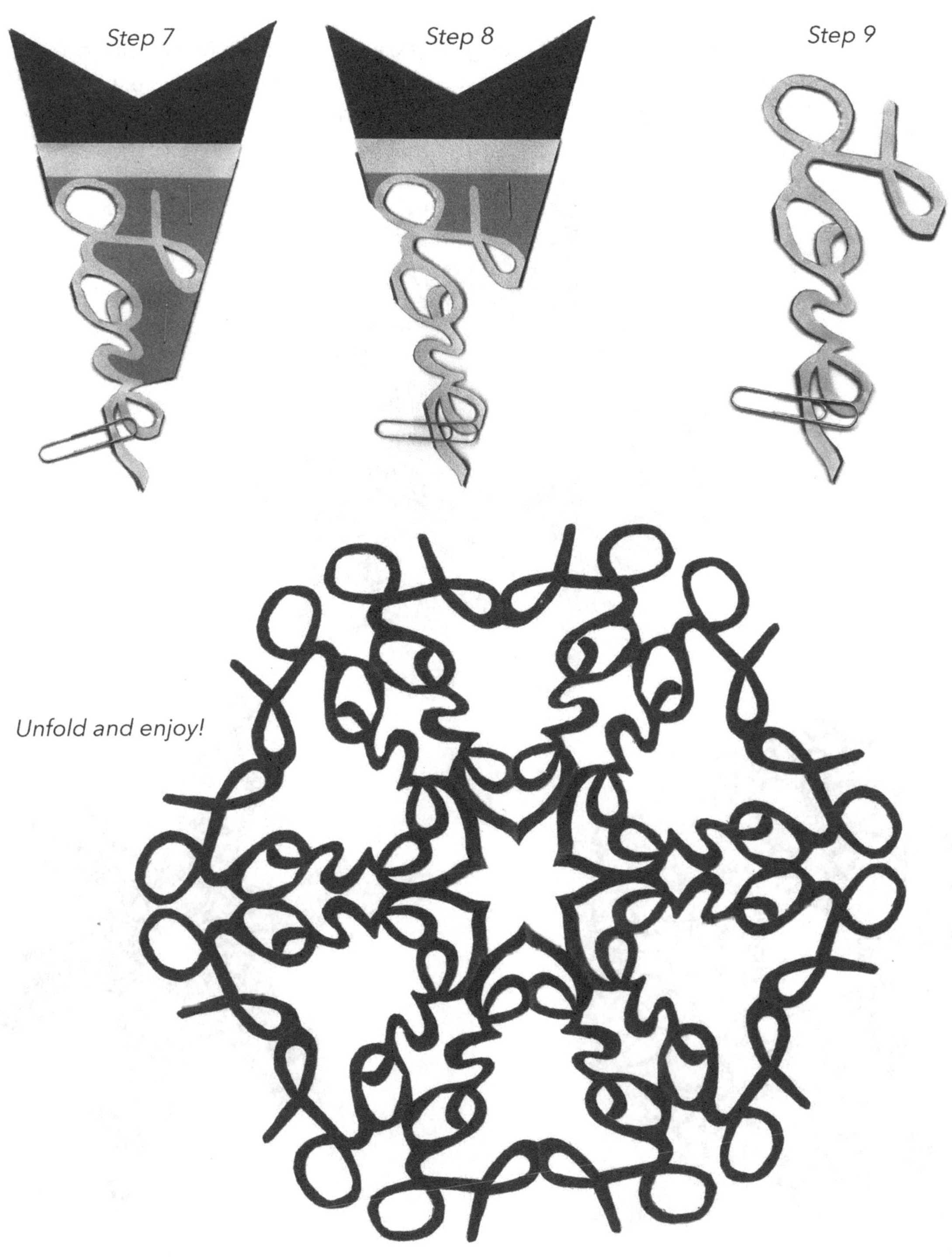

Cutting Snowflakes

GLORIA!!!

WHEN WORDS ALONE FAIL US, we have song to express our joy! As we unite our hearts and voices, heavenly and earthly choirs celebrate the birth of our Savior, Jesus Christ! [See 1 Chronicles: 16: 8-10 (especially 9), D&C 25:12, Colossians 3:16, James 5:13 "Is any merry? Let him sing psalms"]

GLORIA

See pattern on page 86.

Follow along with the steps and their corresponding images below.

Step1: Attach the pattern to the folded paper. Cut away a corner if necessary and then use the hole punch to reach the interior shaded areas. Note: The dashed line shows the possible location of an access cut to access the area between the G and the star. An access cut will make it easier to cut out this snowflake, but it will make the snowflake less stable.

Step 2: Use a small pair of sharp tipped scissors to finish cutting out the inside of the 'O' and 'A.'

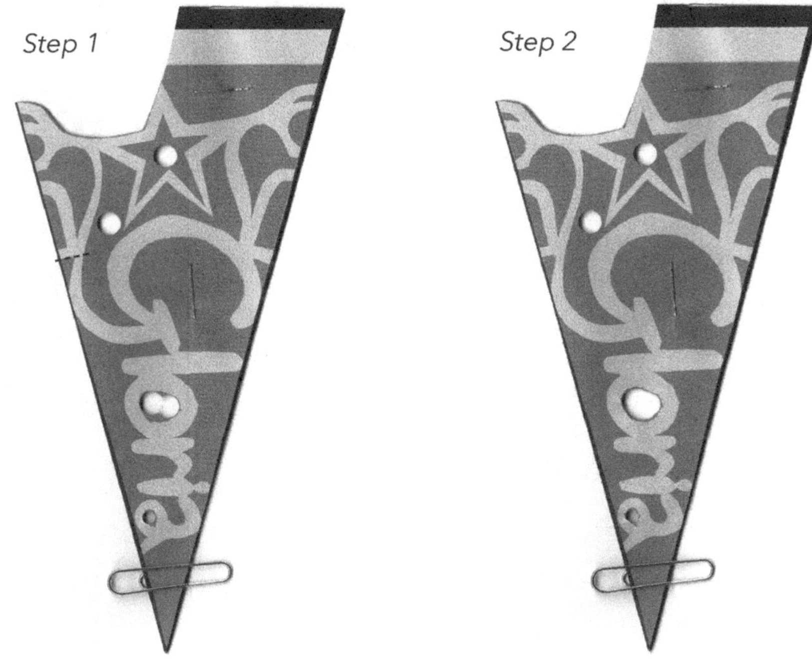

Steps 3–8: Use a small pair of scissors to cut out the inside of the star.

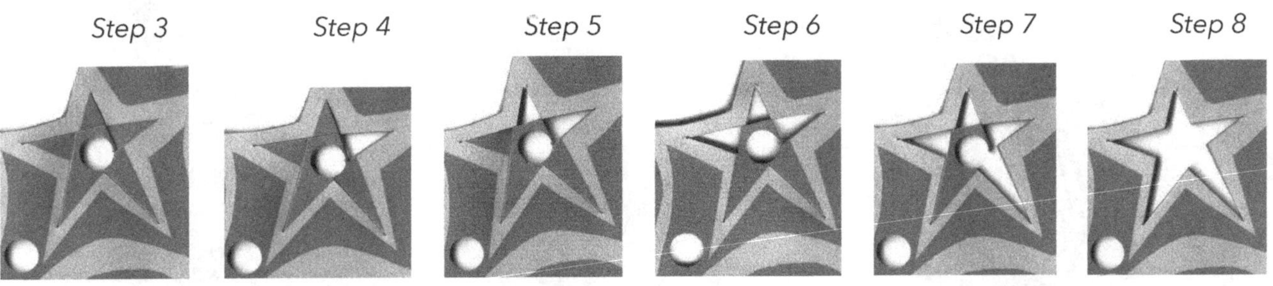

GLORIA (continued)

Follow along with the steps and their corresponding images below.

Steps 9–11: Using a pair of small, sharp tipped scissors, carefully remove the shaded area between the star and the 'G.'

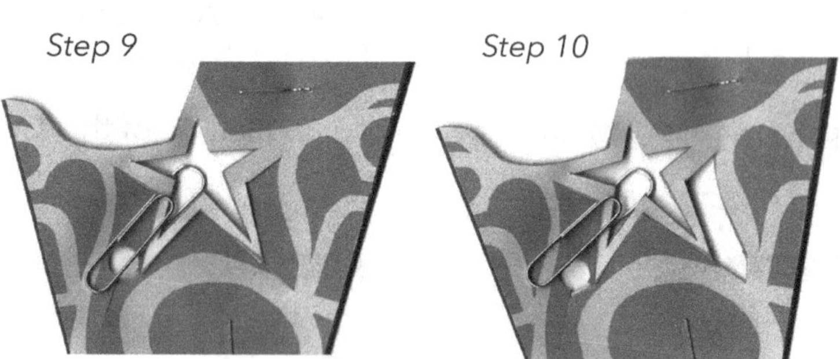

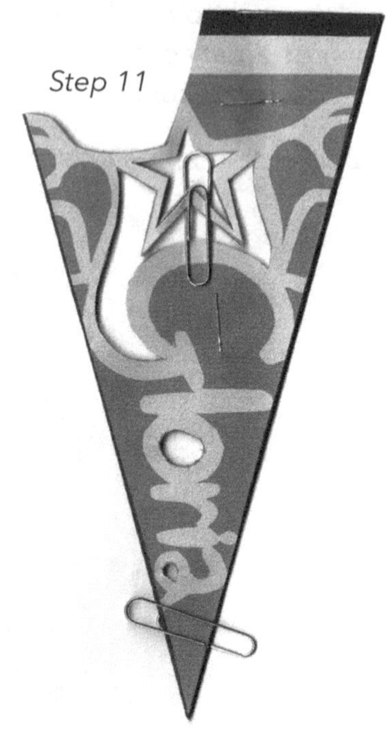

Steps 12–16: Cut out the angels. Start with the head, then the halo, wings, and body. Remove the shaded area under the angels.

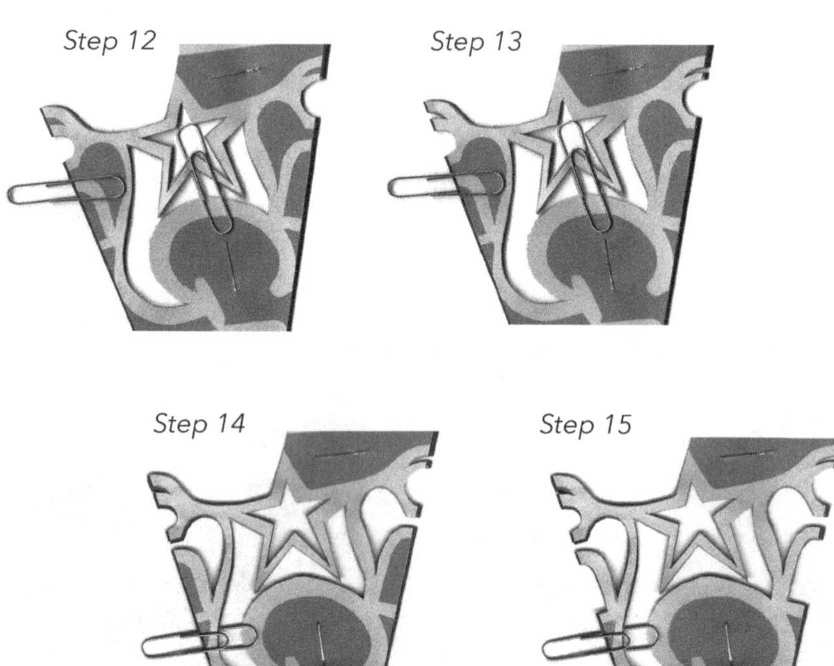

Steps 17–20: Remove the shaded areas from the more complicated side of 'Gloria' first, dividing it into more manageable pieces to help prevent shifting and to make cutting easier. Leave the stapled interior of 'G' until later for stability.

Steps 21–22: Remove the remaining shaded area. Unfold and enjoy!

Unfold and enjoy!

CHOIR

*See pattern on page 82.

Follow along with the steps and their corresponding images below.

Steps 1-4: Use a hole punch to start the interior space. Use a small pair of sharp tipped scissors to expand the opening being careful to stay in the shaded area. As you are able, begin cutting along the lines: down along the arm, and across the top of the music (as shown in the second picture from the left.) If you have an XL hole punch, you can use it for the head, but the illustrations above show how it can be done with scissors.

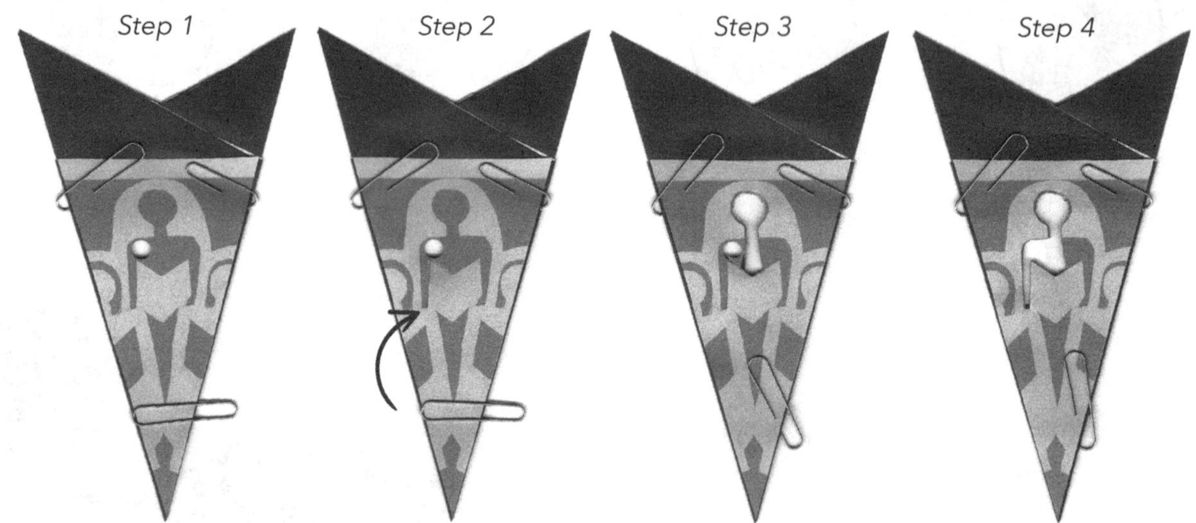

Steps 5-8: Between the shoulder and the music is an access cut to reach the remaining interior space [See arrow]. Continue removing the shaded areas, working toward the center.

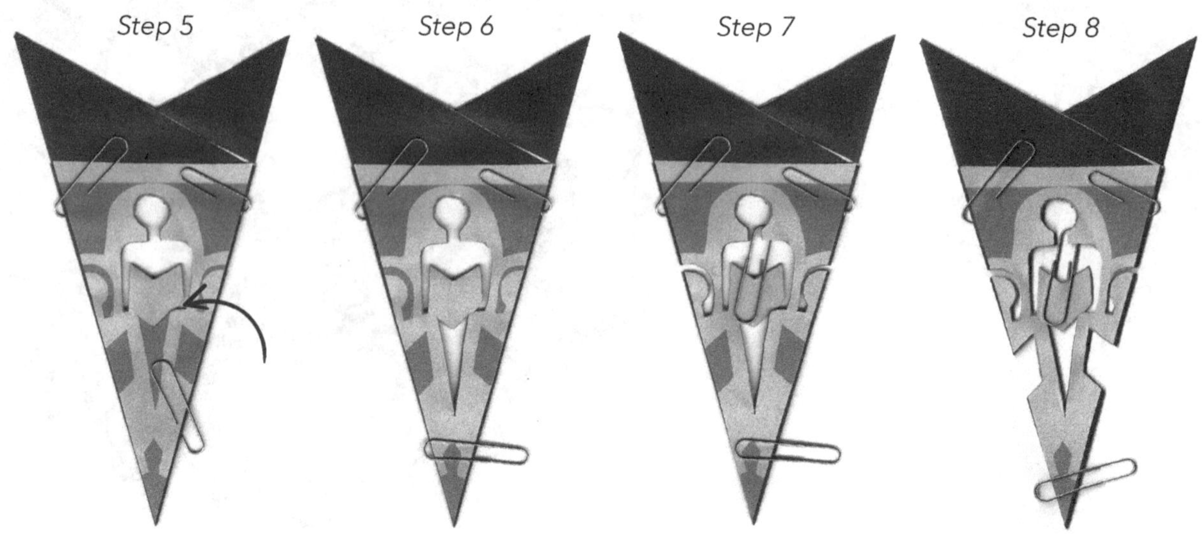

TIP: Add paper clips for stability to prevent layers from sliding apart.

Step 9: Cut out the center.

Step 10: Cut away the remaining shaded area on the outside edge. Unfold and enjoy!

Step 9

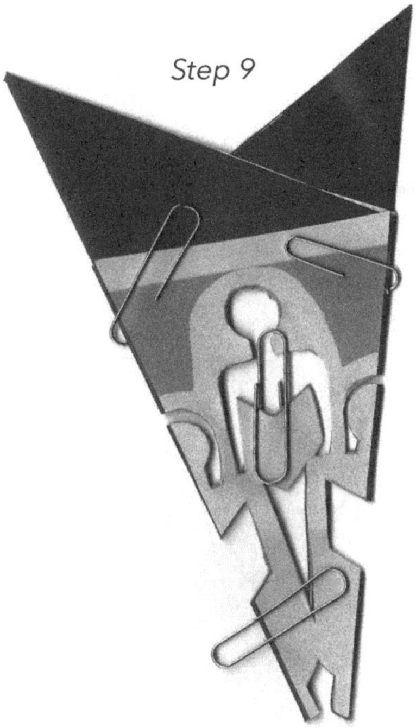

Step 10

Unfold and enjoy!

CHOIR WITH BELL TOWER

See pattern on page 87.

Follow along with the steps and their corresponding images below.

Step 1: Attach the pattern to the folded paper and punch out the central choir member's head.

Step 2: Use a small pair of sharp-tipped scissors to cut along the neck.

Step 3: Extend the cut line along one arm.

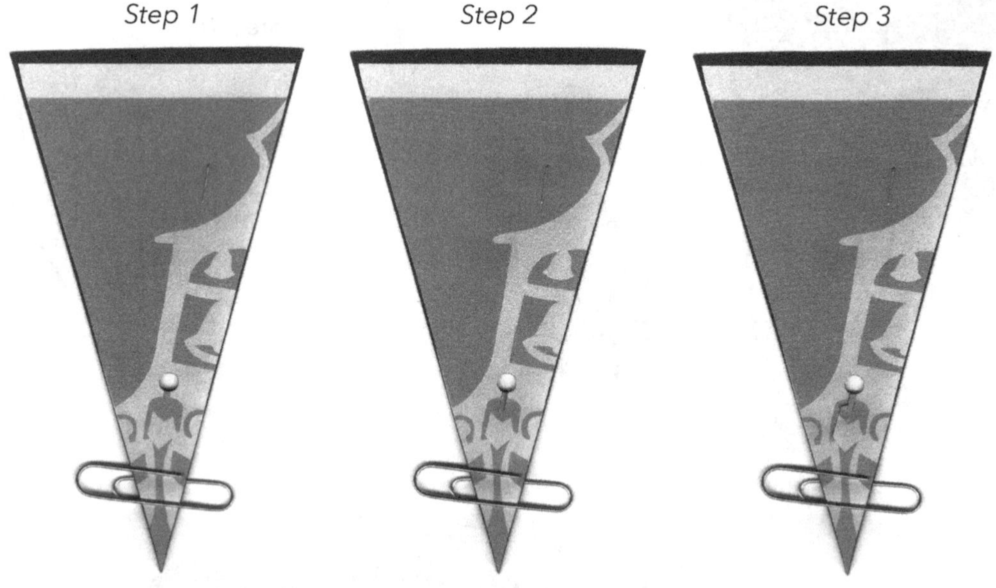

Step 4: Cut along the top of the music and over to the other arm. Divide the shaded area into more parts if needed.

Step 5: Finish cutting out the arm.

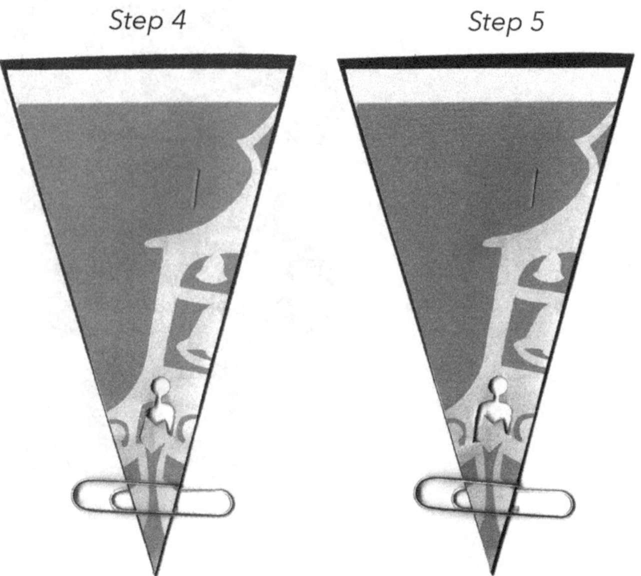

Steps 6–8: Create the diamond in the steeple and reveal the upper bell in two parts.

Step 6 *Step 7* *Step 8*

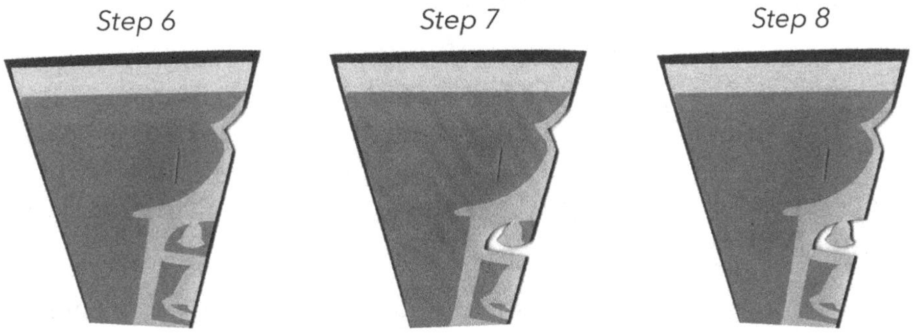

Steps 9–14: Continue to remove the shaded areas of the pattern leaving the outer portion until the end. Unfold and enjoy!

Step 9 *Step 10* *Step 11* *Step 12* *Step 13*

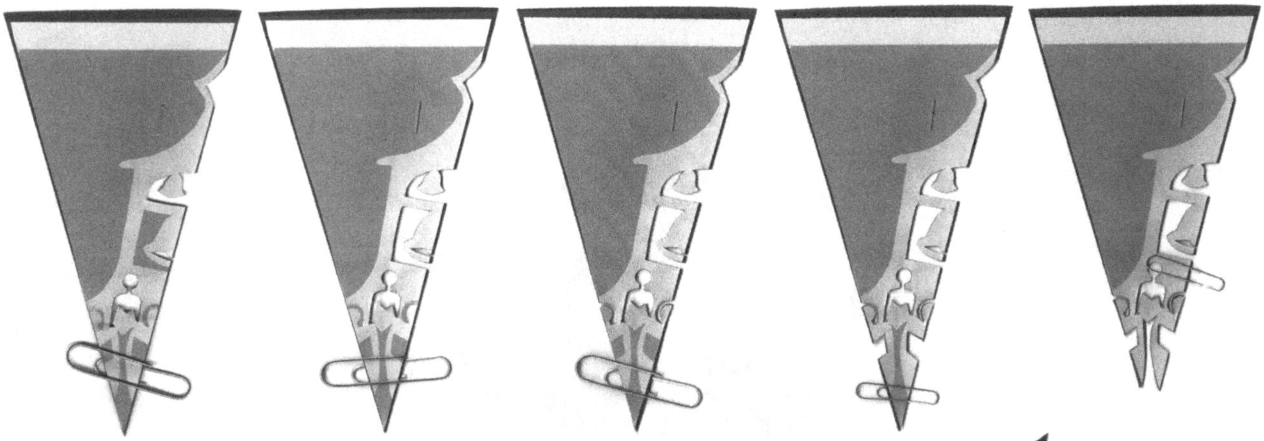

Step 14

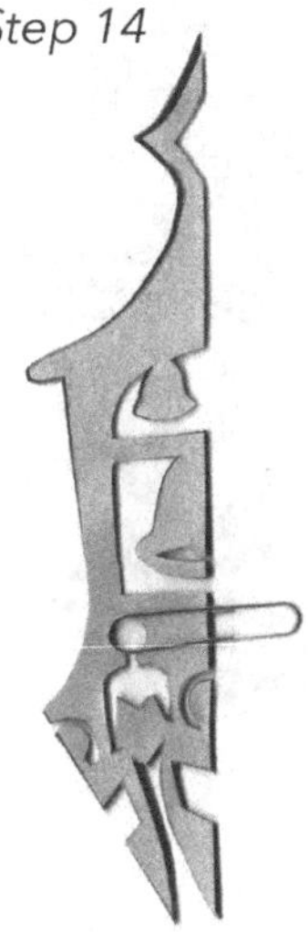

Unfold and enjoy!

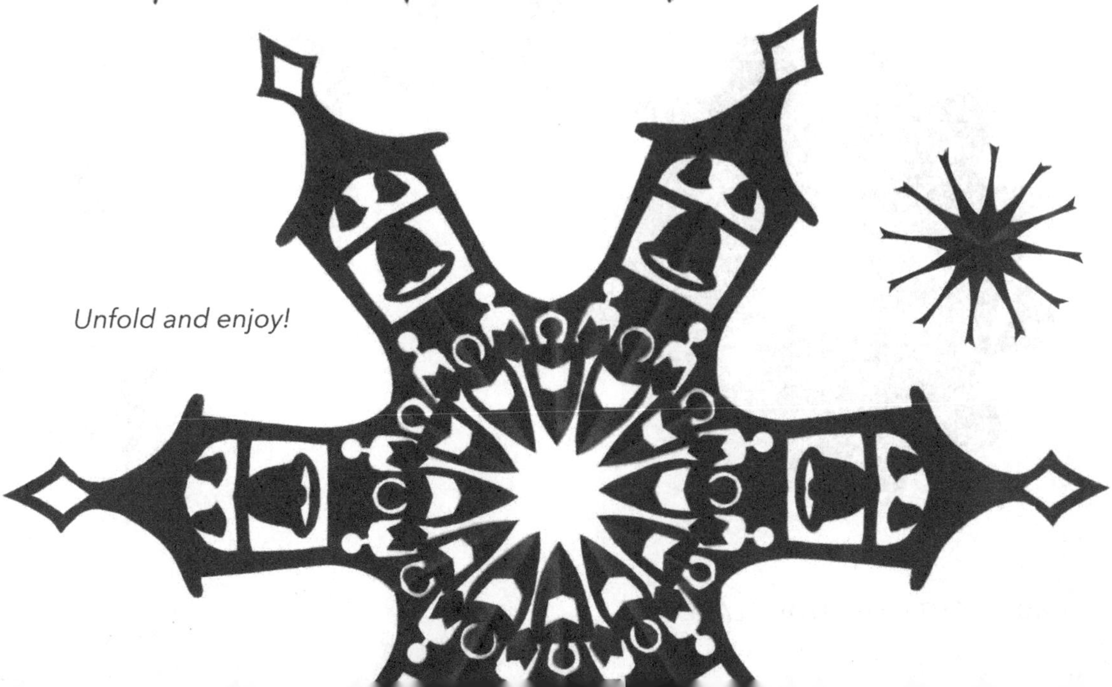

Cutting Snowflakes

HANDBELL CHOIR

HANDBELL CHOIRS ARE A MUSICAL TREAT found primarily at Christmas time, performing in churches and on street corners.

Even out the central figure's vest if you must, but the uneven vest gives a sense of motion to the finished snowflake.

Interior spaces are becoming more challenging. Hole punches are a good starting point, but sometimes a different approach is better. Interior spaces can be reached by making an access cut from the outside [See the bowtie and hair of the bell ringer bottom left and on page 83]. Try to make access cuts thin, so they will be less noticeable on the finished snowflake. Be mindful of how access cuts will affect the finished snowflake.

BOWTIES AND BELLS

**See pattern on page 83.*

TIPS: This one definitely looks different on dark paper vs light!

- This snowflake will challenge your access cut skills as it uses a series of access cuts to reach the hair.
- A small pair of sharp tipped scissors works well in this instance.

Follow along with the steps and their corresponding images below.

Step 1: Start by cutting away the shaded area above the bell.

Step 2: The access cut goes up from the bell to the shoulder. Cut out the bow tie and shoulder areas.

Step 3: The access cut goes from the corner of the bow tie along the side of his face to reach his hair. Cut out his hair.

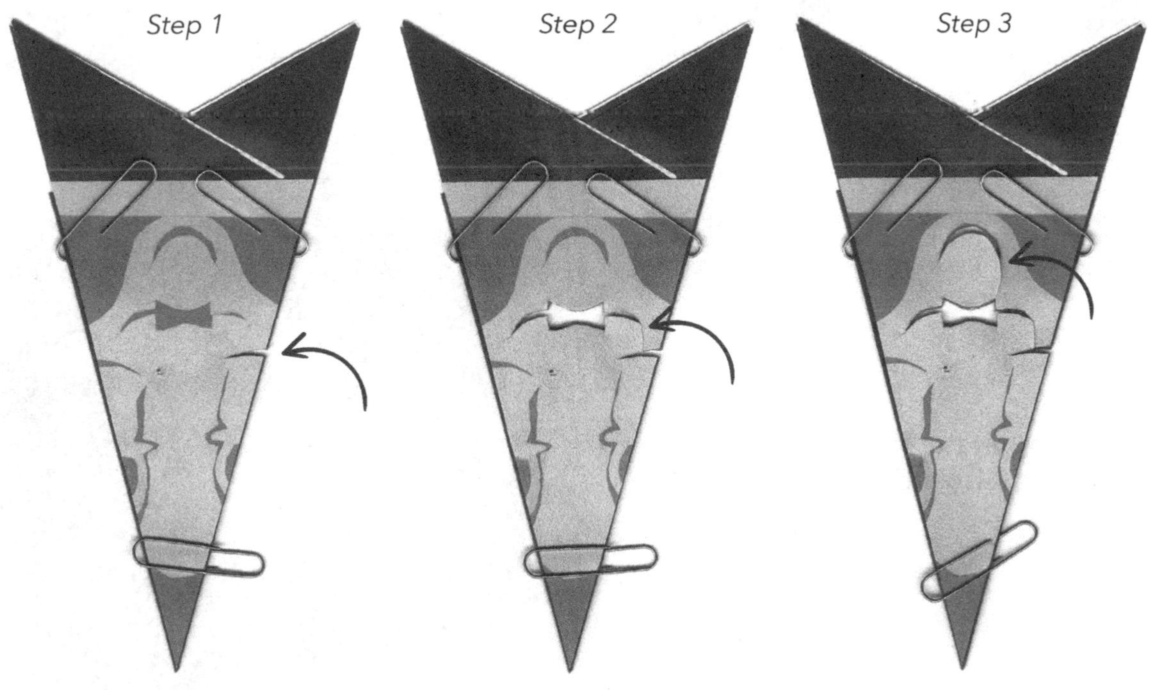

BOWTIES AND BELLS (continued)

Steps 4–9: Continue cutting away the shaded areas of the pattern, working your way toward the middle.

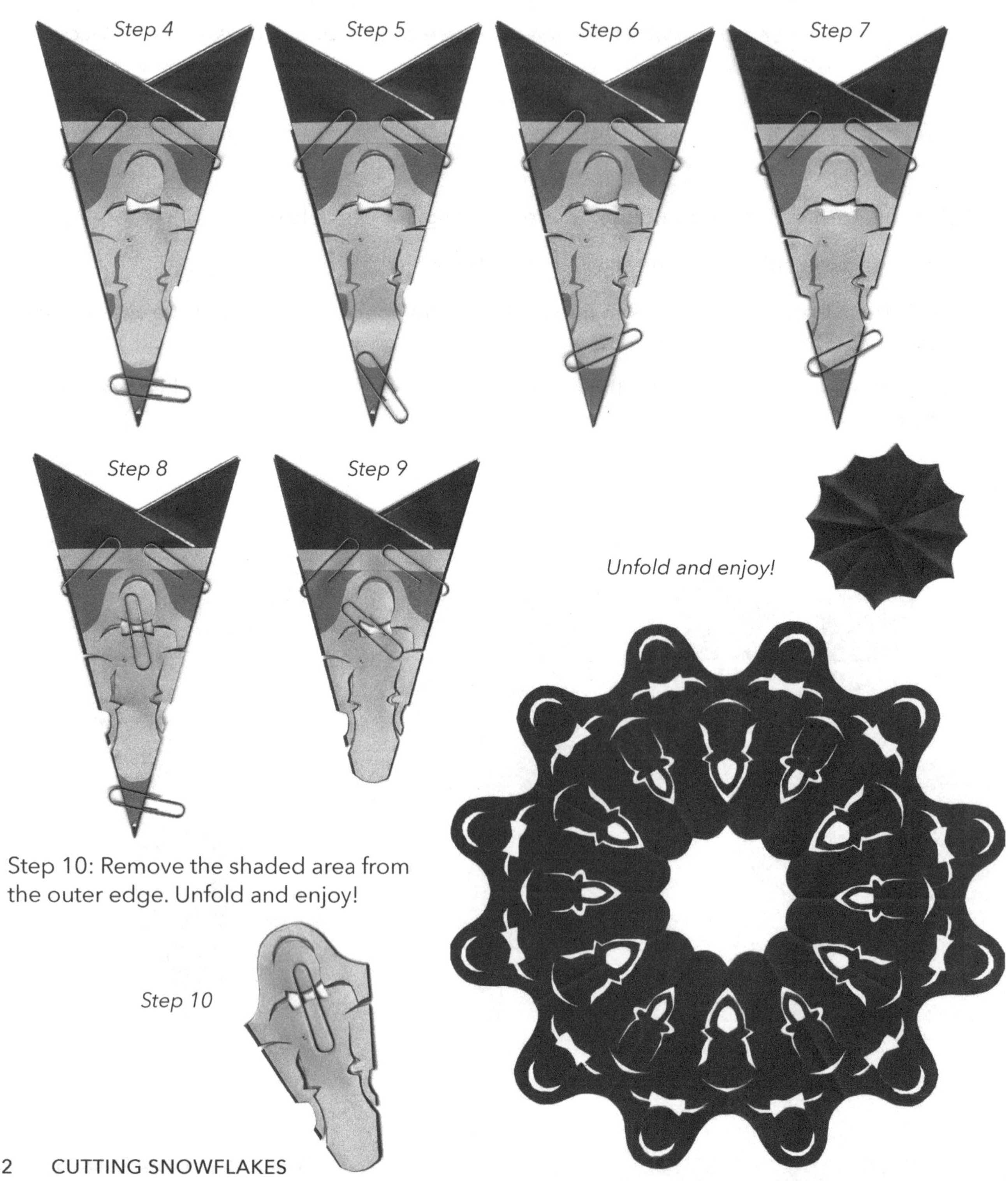

Step 10: Remove the shaded area from the outer edge. Unfold and enjoy!

HANDBELL CHOIR

**See pattern on page 83.*

Follow along with the steps and their corresponding images below.

Steps 1-8: Use a hole punch to start the interior space: the vest. Using a small pair of sharp tipped scissors, start making cuts within the shaded area. Break the space into manageable pieces, being patient with yourself and the process.

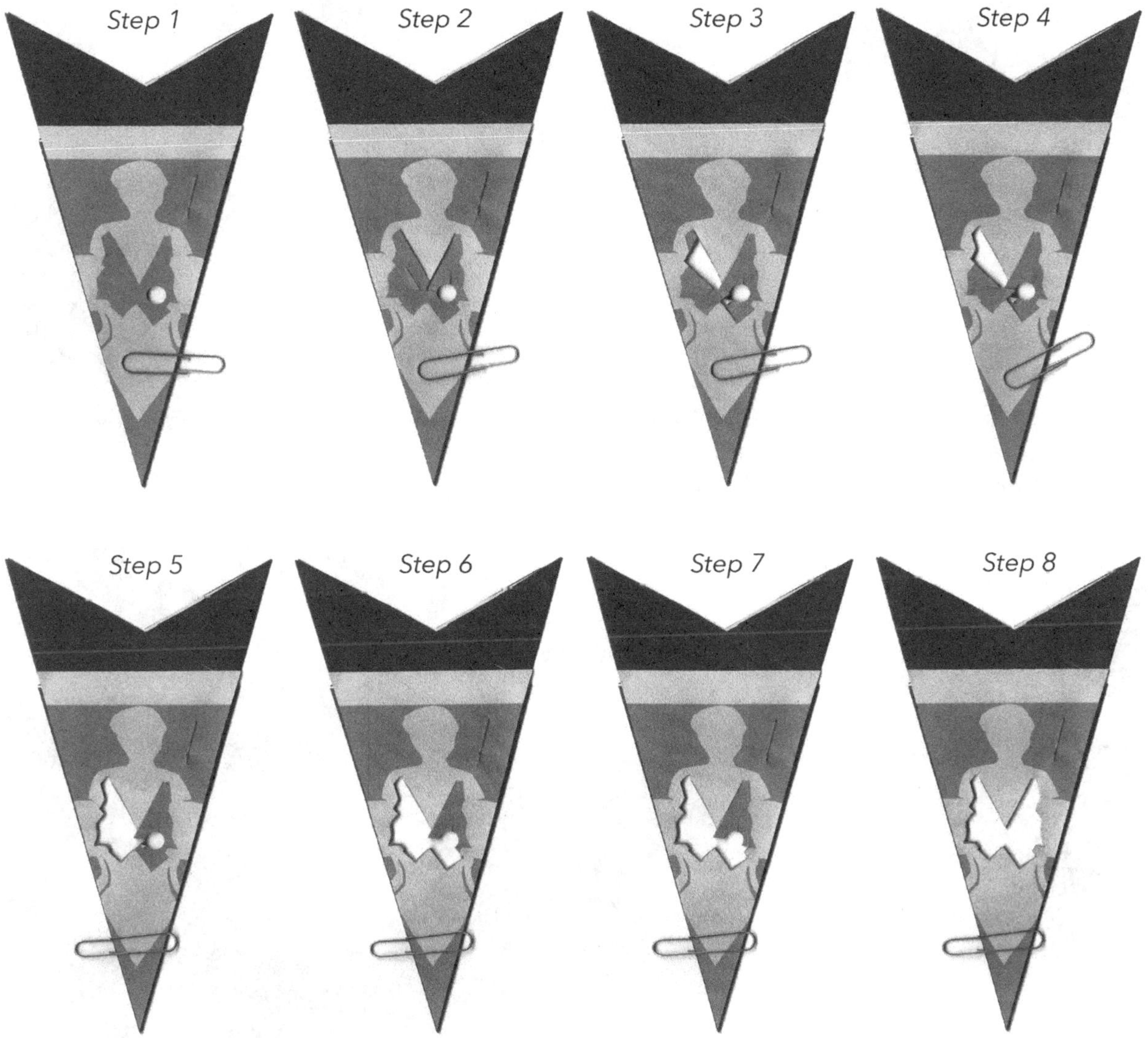

Step 1

Step 2

Step 3

Step 4

Step 5

Step 6

Step 7

Step 8

TIP: If you choose, you can make an access cut along the top of one of the bells.

HANDBELL CHOIR (continued)

Steps 9-11: Continue cutting away the shaded areas, working toward the center.

Steps 12-13: Small cuts can be used to make the sharp cuts above the bells before removing the remaining shaded area. Unfold and enjoy!

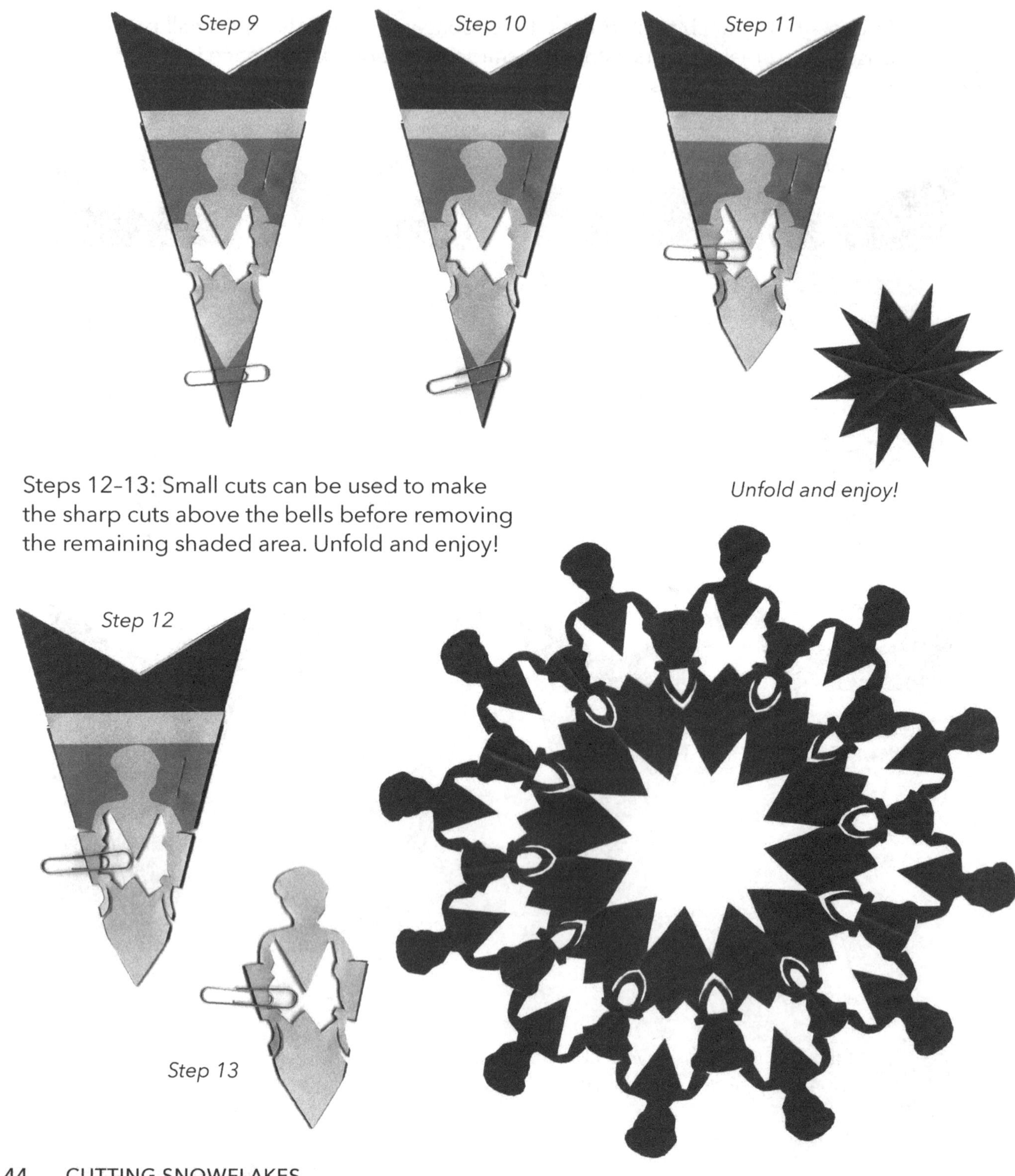

HANDBELL CHOIR WITH BELL TOWER

**See pattern on page 87.*

Follow along with the steps and their corresponding images below.

Steps 1–8: In order to use the hole punch in interior spaces, cut away the shaded areas as necessary. Make cuts within the shaded areas to allow room to make the final cuts.

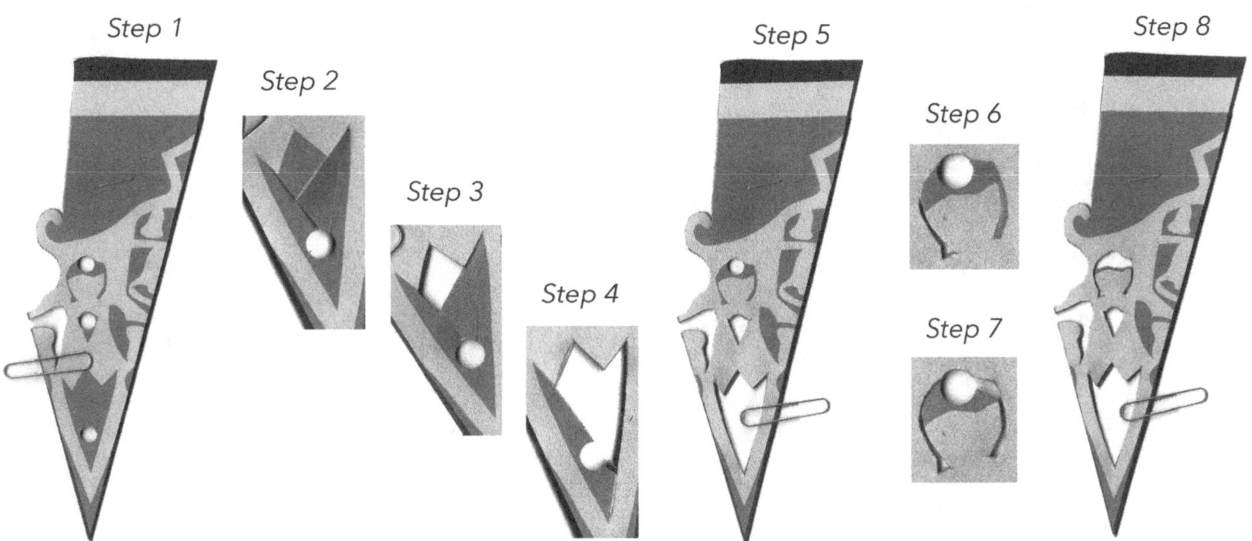

Steps 9–15: Continue to cut away the shaded areas, working toward the center. Leave the stapled area on the outer edge until last for stability. Use multiple paper clips to stabilize the paper as you are cutting, especially if you are using a slick paper.

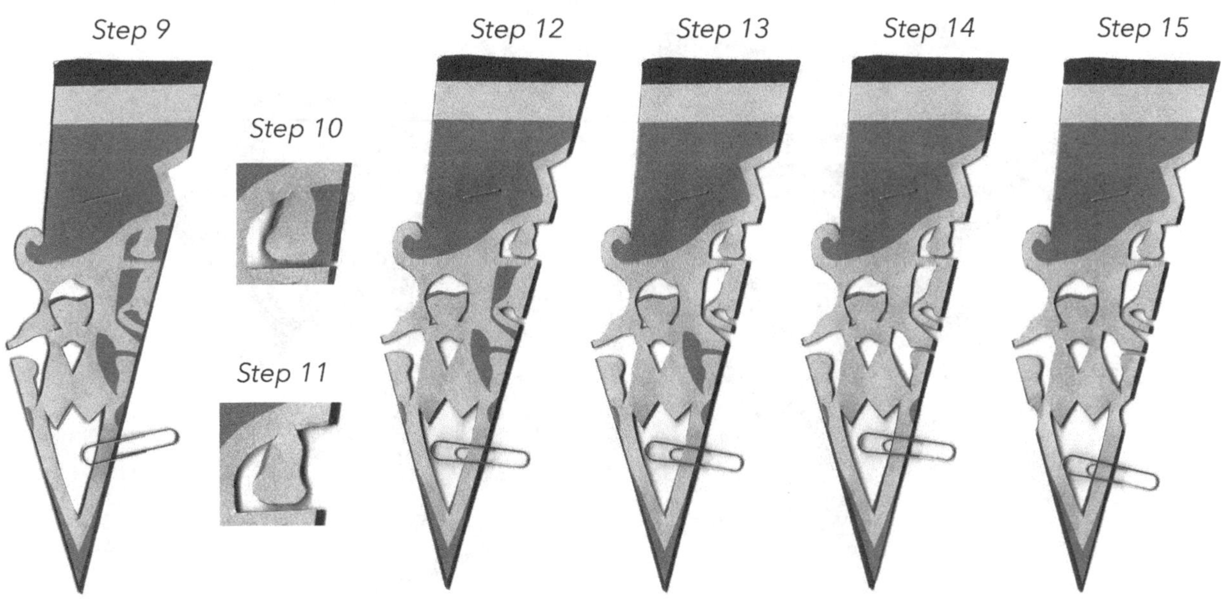

HANDBELL CHOIR WITH BELL TOWER (continued)

Step 16: Remove Center

Step 17: Remove the remaining portion of the outer edge. A small pair of scissors is useful for the Curly-Q. Unfold and enjoy!

Step 16

Step 17

Unfold and enjoy!

BONUS PATTERN: DONKEY

**See pattern on page 85.*

Follow along with the steps and their corresponding images below.

Step 1: Attach the pattern to the folded paper, punch out the eye, and cut out the mouth.

Step 2: Cut out the detail in the cheek

Step 3: Finish cutting out the center. Enjoy the two-in-one as is, or add more detail as desired.

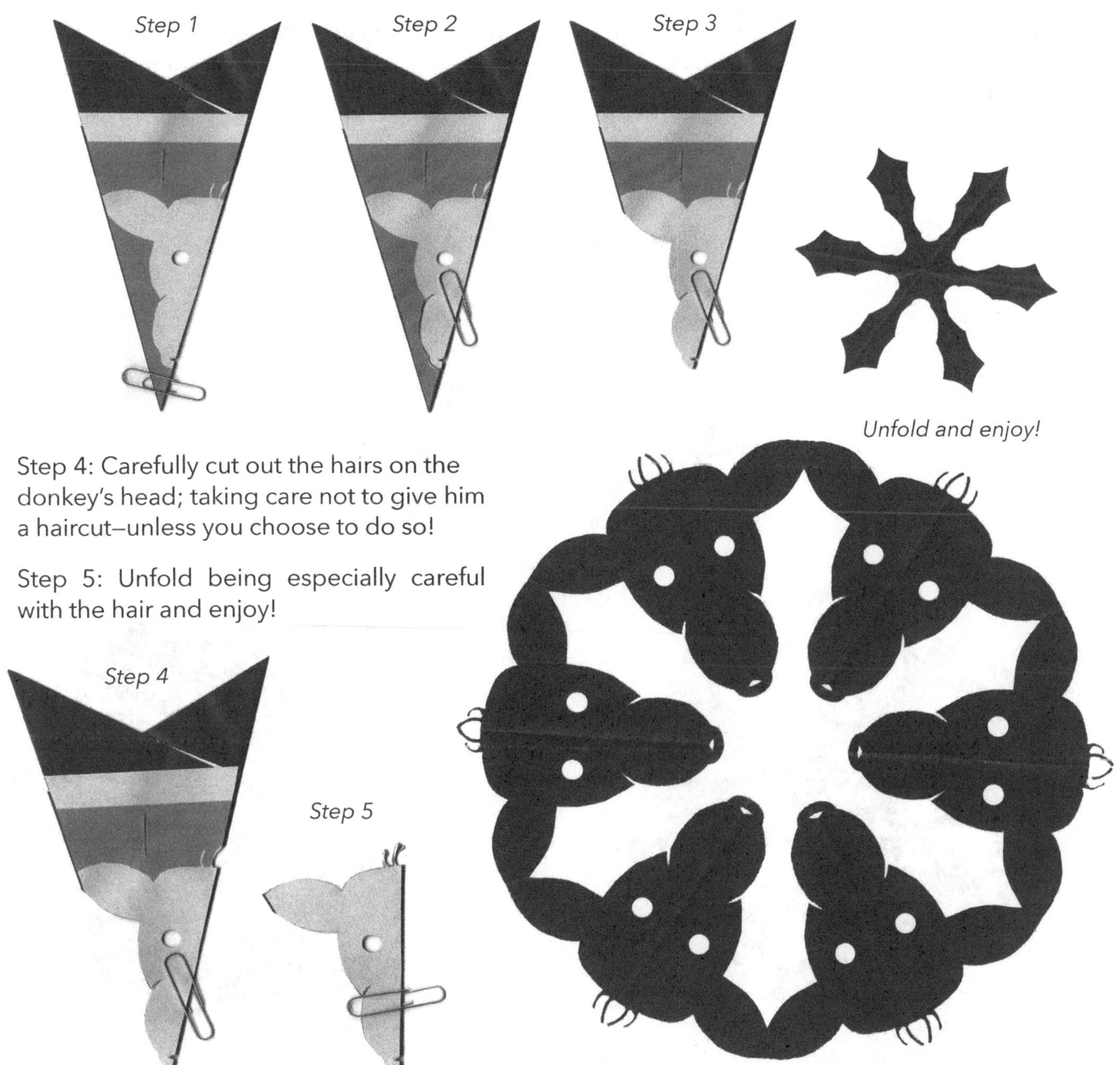

Step 4: Carefully cut out the hairs on the donkey's head; taking care not to give him a haircut–unless you choose to do so!

Step 5: Unfold being especially careful with the hair and enjoy!

Cutting Snowflakes

LOVE ONE ANOTHER

CHRISTMAS TIME IS WHEN we remember best the commandment, from John 15:12 "Love one another, as I have loved you." [See John 13:34-35, Matthew 22:37-40, Mosiah 18:8-11, 4:14-16 "Teach them to love one another, and to serve one another"]

The snowflake pattern on the lower left is reminiscent of Daddy Daughter Dances. While the center snowflake reminds us that everyone big and small can join together to better our communities and world.

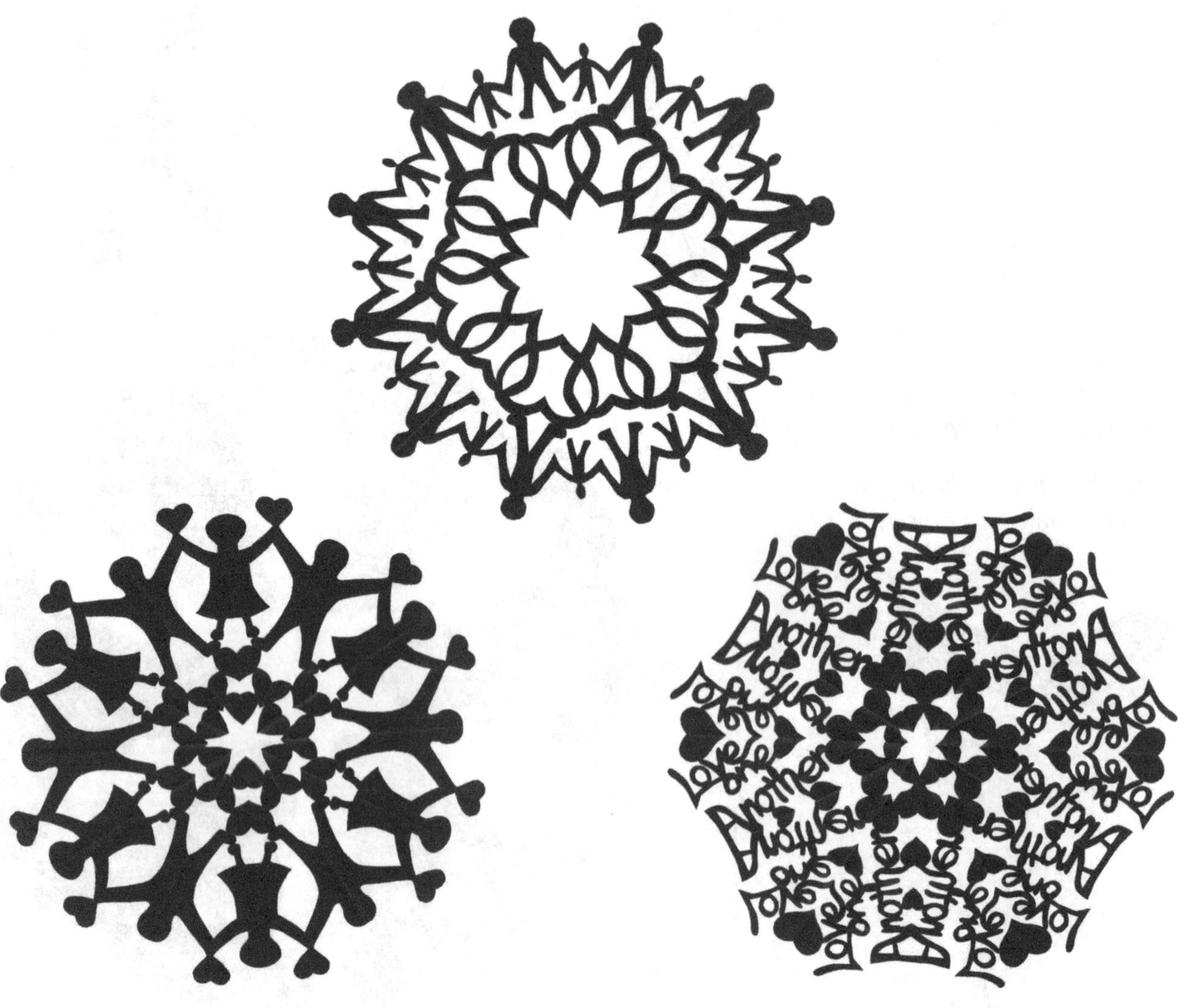

DADDY DAUGHTER DANCE

**See pattern on page 83.*

Follow along with the steps and their corresponding images below.

Steps 1–4: To remove the interior, use an access cut: start at the top of the heart and go between the feet [See arrow]. Continue cutting away the shaded portion, working toward the center.

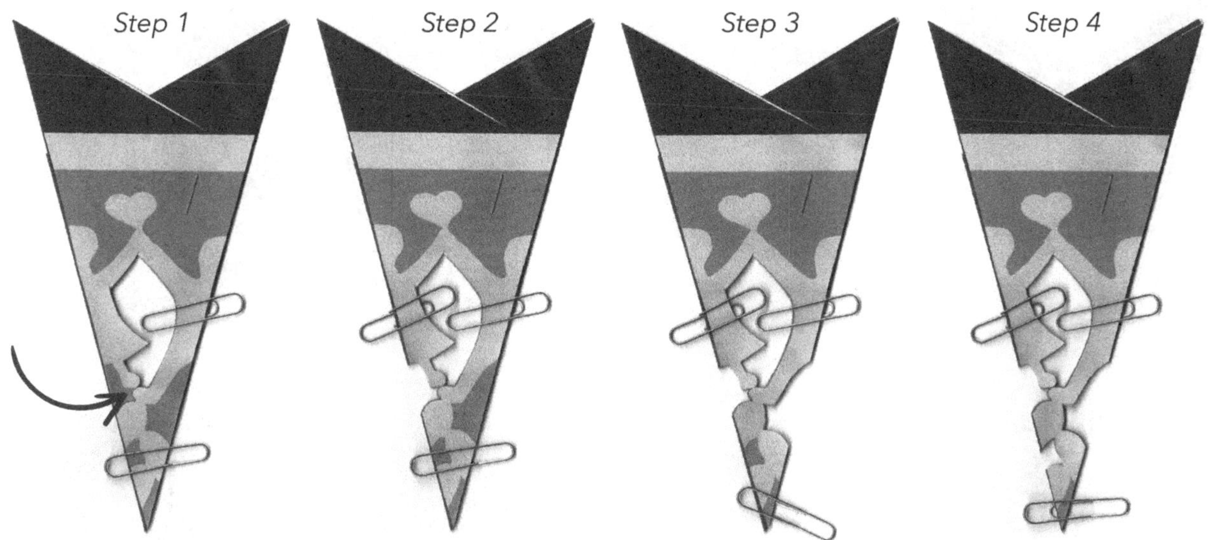

Step 5: Remove the center.

Step 6: Finish cutting away the outside. Unfold and enjoy!

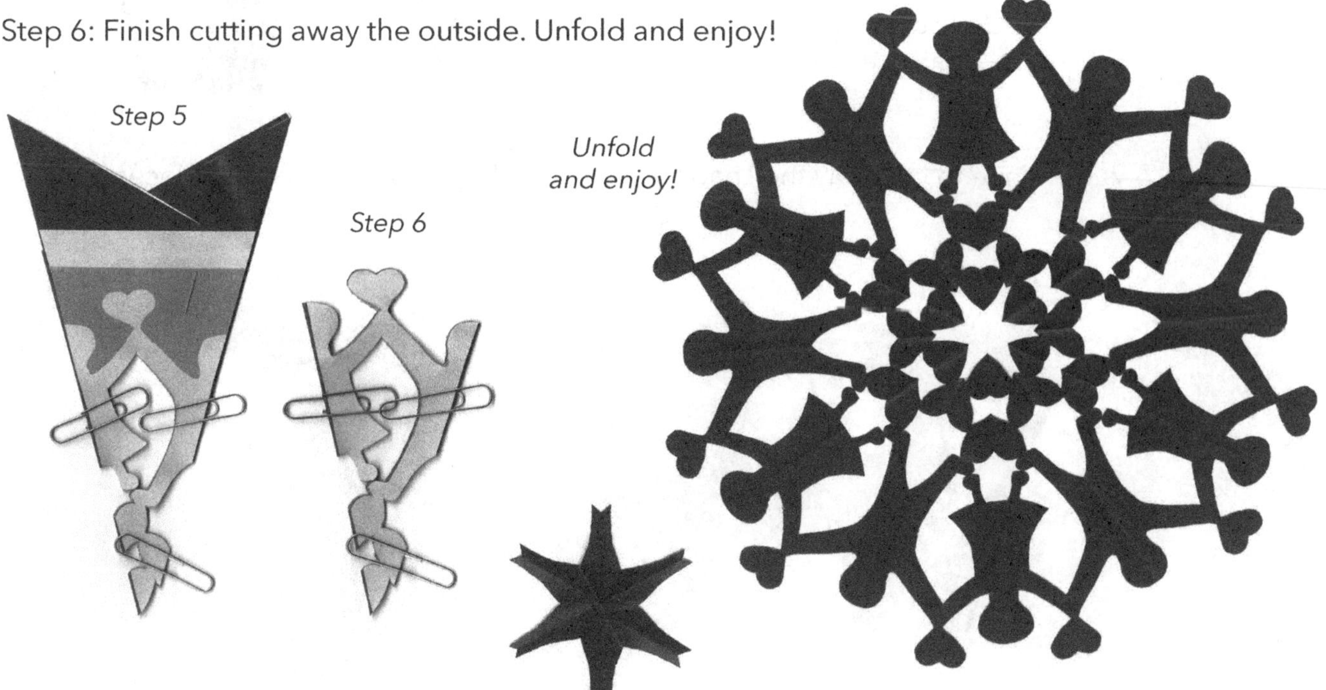

HOLDING HANDS

**See pattern on page 84.*

Follow along with the steps and their corresponding images below.

Steps 1-6: Use a paper punch to start the interior space. Divide the complicated shaded area into more manageable pieces.

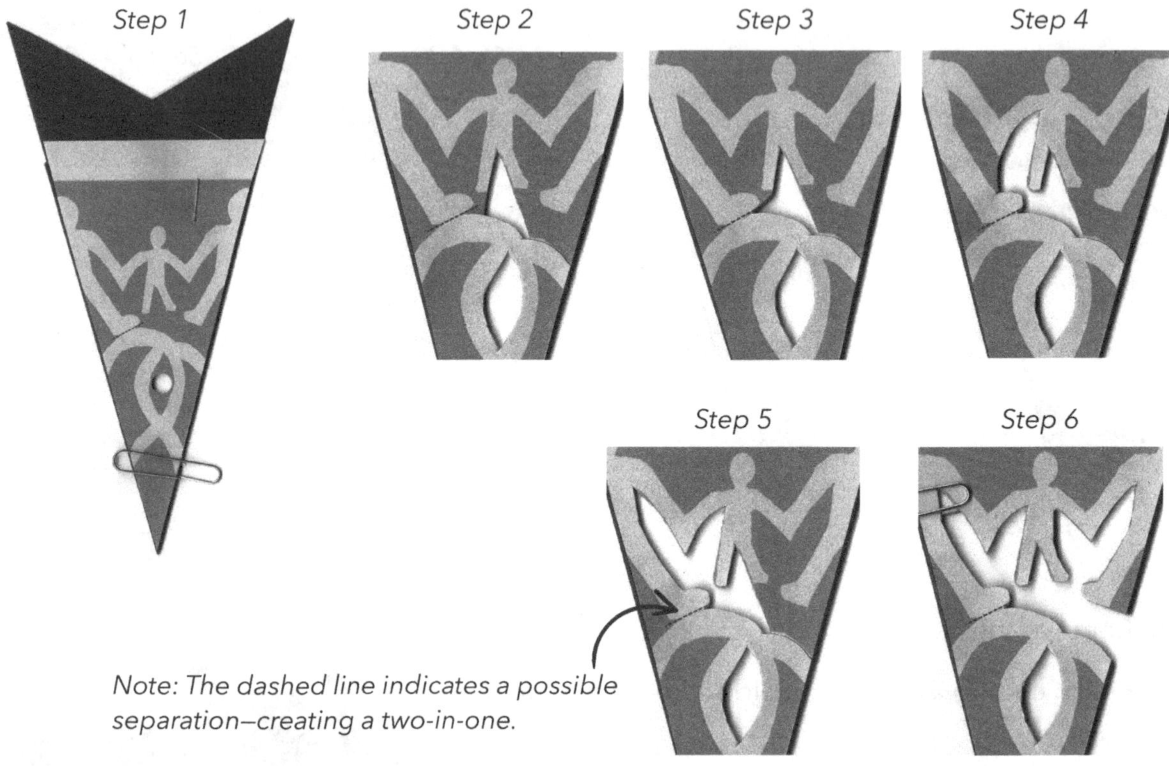

Steps 7-9: Continue to cut away the shaded areas, dividing into manageable pieces as needed.

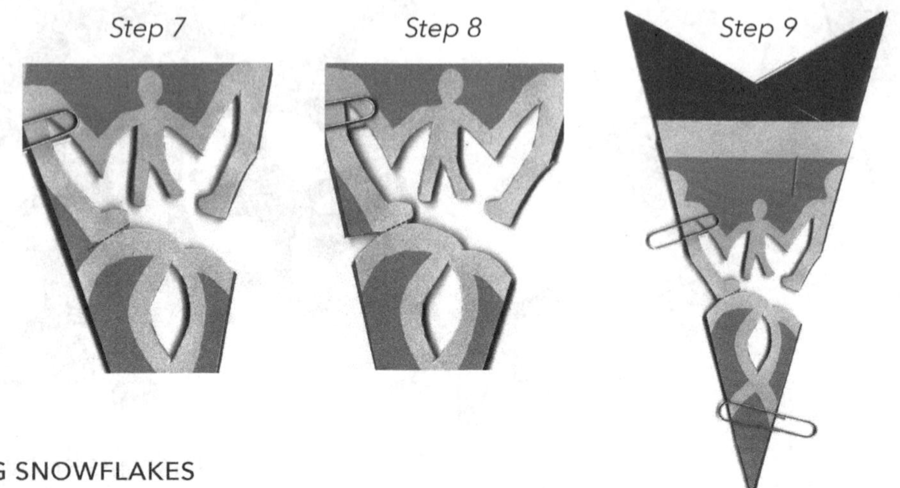

Steps 10–12: Continue cutting away the shaded areas, working your way toward the center.

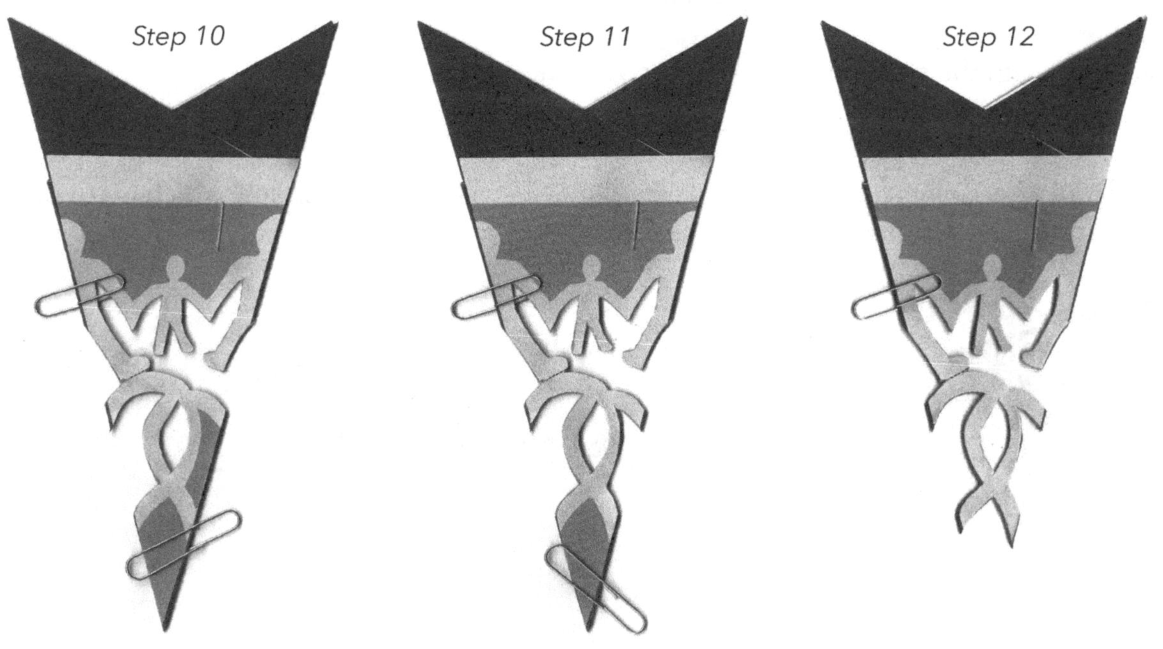

Step 13: Remove the remaining shaded area from the outer edge of the pattern. Unfold and enjoy!

Step 13

Unfold and enjoy!

LOVE ONE ANOTHER

**See pattern on page 88.*

Follow along with the steps and their corresponding images below.

Step 1: Use a ⅛″ hole punch to start the interior spaces.

Step 2: The arrow points to an access cut used to access an interior space, which is cut out in order to use the hole punch in the 'o' in 'one.'

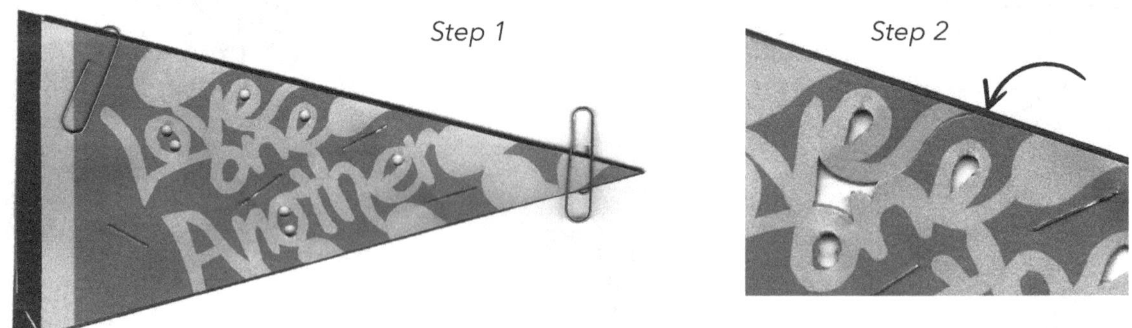

Steps 3-7: Try to work on the areas that are not stabilized by staples first. Staples are highly recommended to prevent shifting.

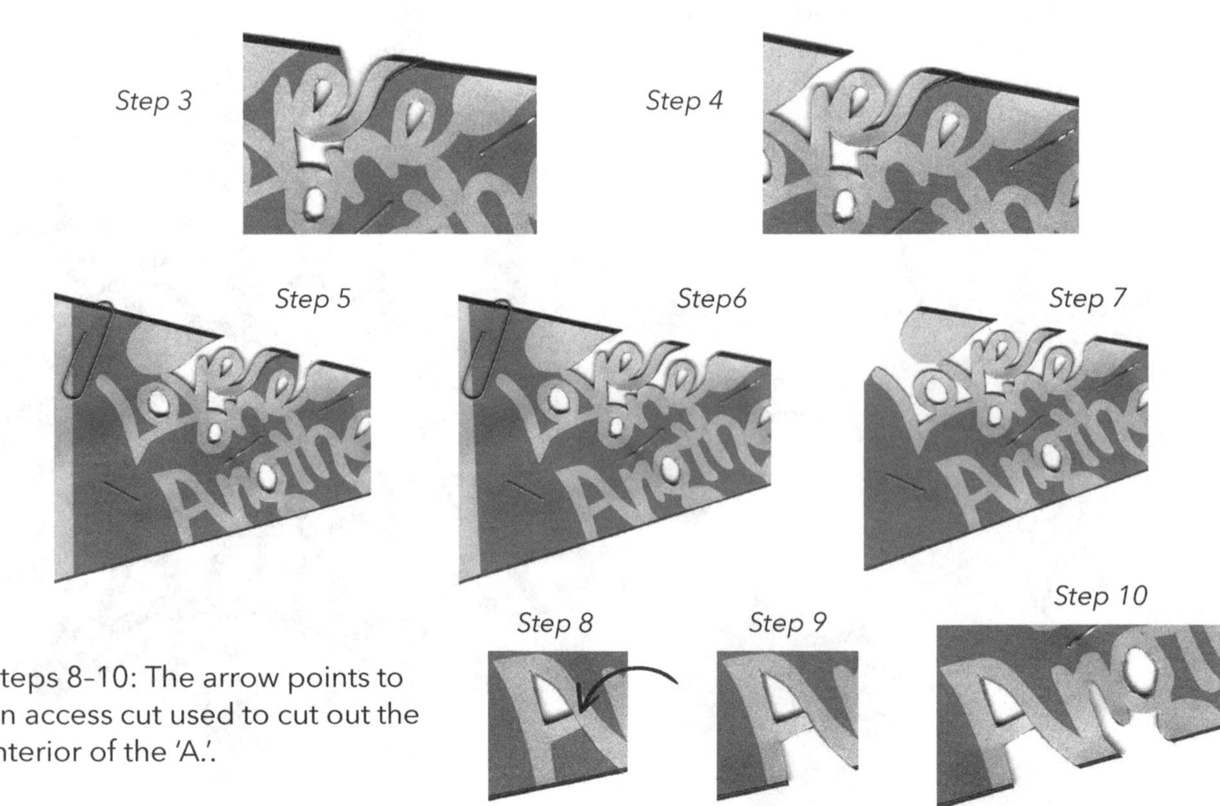

Steps 8-10: The arrow points to an access cut used to cut out the interior of the 'A.'.

Steps 11–14: Continue cutting away the shaded area.

Step 15: The arrow points to an access cut.

Step 11

Step 12

Step 13

Step 14

Step 15

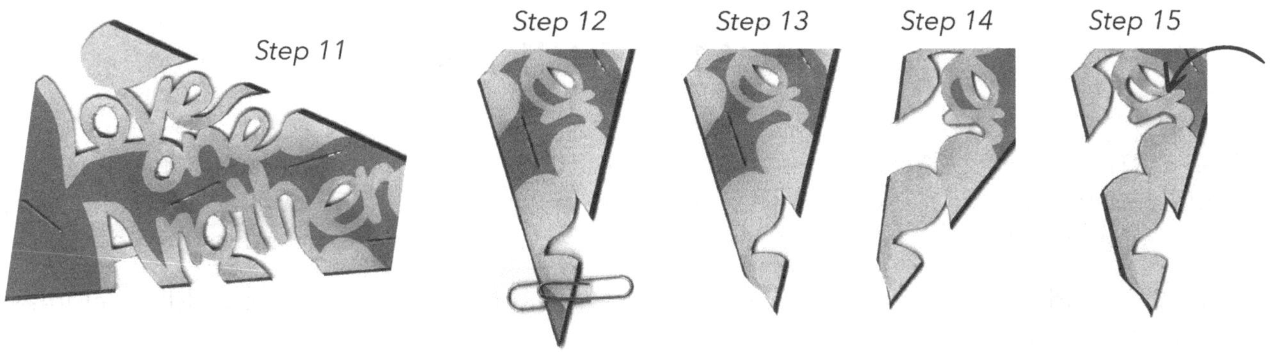

Steps 16–18: Try to leave the staples as long as possible for stability.

Steps 19–20: Finish cutting away the shaded area. Unfold and enjoy!

Step 16

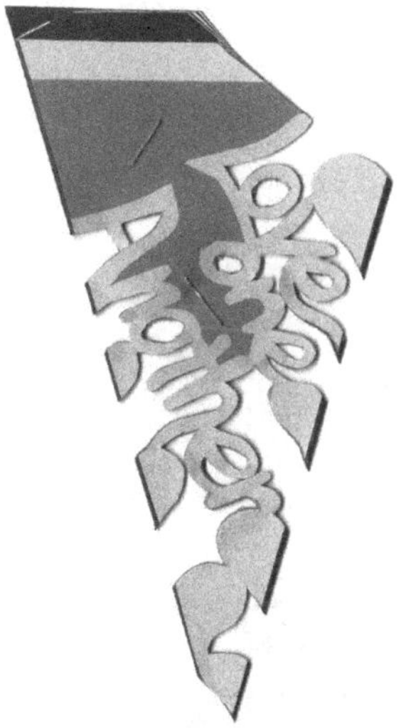

Step 17

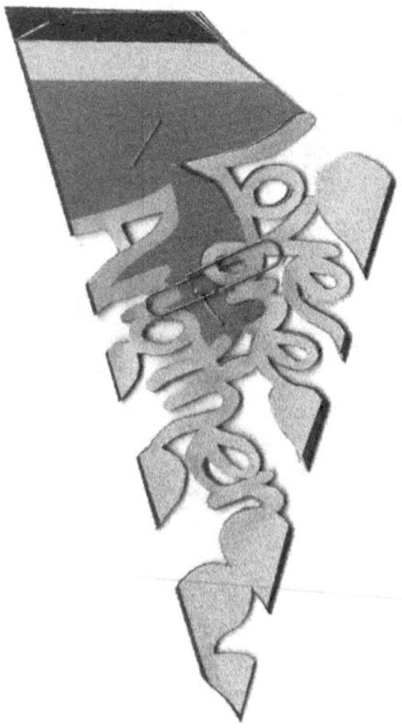

Step 18

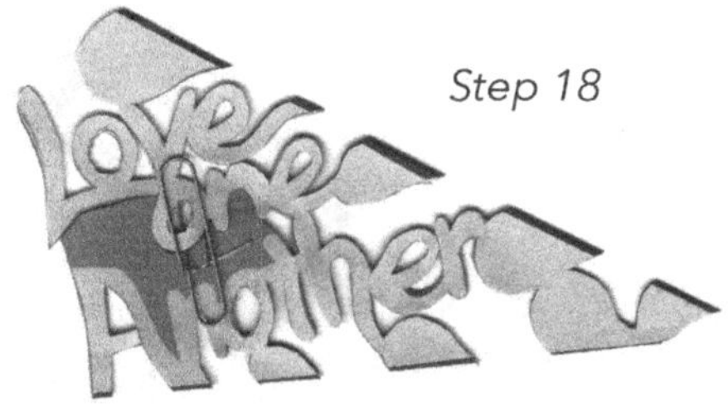

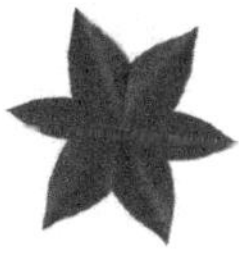

Step 19

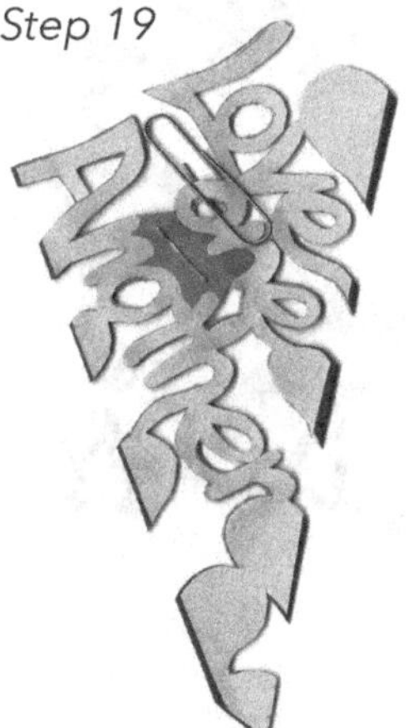

Step 20

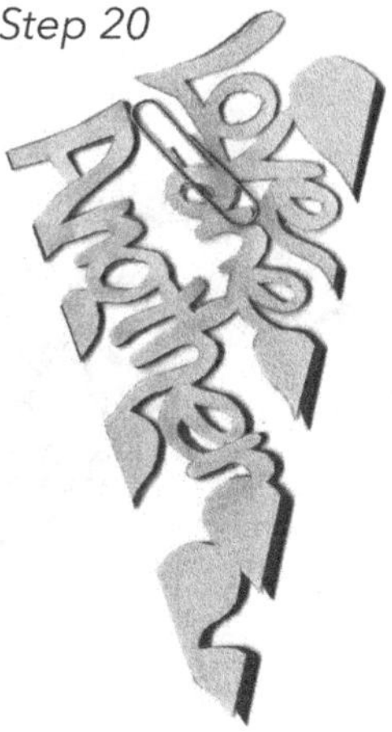

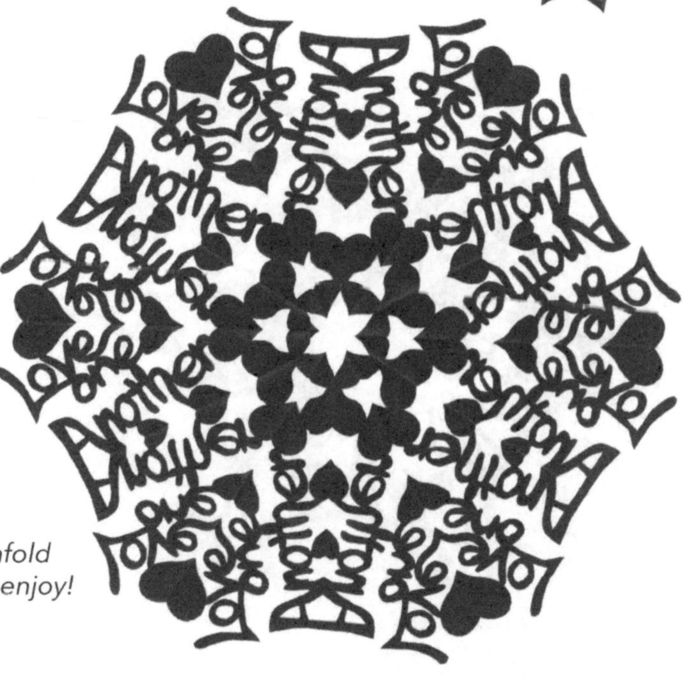

Unfold and enjoy!

Cutting Snowflakes

HUMBLE BIRTH

THE BIRTH OF OUR LORD AND SAVIOR, JESUS CHRIST, is a singular event, but its effects are multiplied throughout our lives. We focus on the Savior's birth during one month of the year; how much more blessed would we be if we focused on Christ every month of the year!

Luke 2:7 "And she brought forth her firstborn son, and wrapped him in swaddling clothes, and laid him in a manger; because there was no room for them in the inn."

HUMBLE BIRTH

**See pattern on page 88.*

Follow along with the steps and their corresponding images below.

Steps 1–7: Remove the shaded areas, dividing the complex areas into smaller parts, as needed.

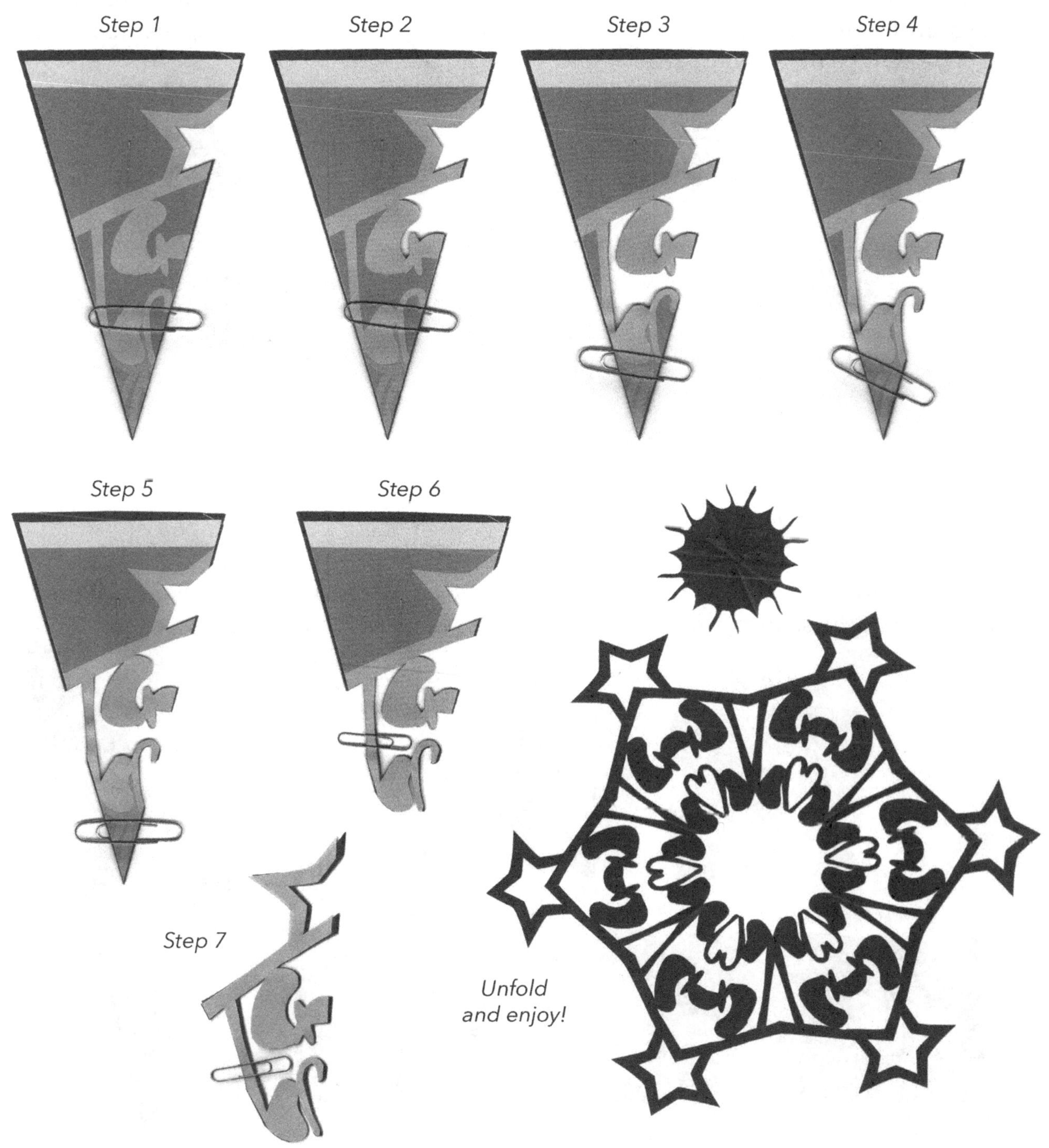

HUMBLE BIRTH - INTERIOR PRACTICE

See pattern on page 84.

Follow along with the steps and their corresponding images below.

Steps 1-3: Attach the pattern to the folded paper. Remove part of the shaded area so the hole punch will reach the interior of the star. Use the hole punch to start all of the interior spaces. Use a small pair of sharp tipped scissors to finish cutting out the interior spaces [See Gloria on page 33 for a more thorough example of cutting out a star].

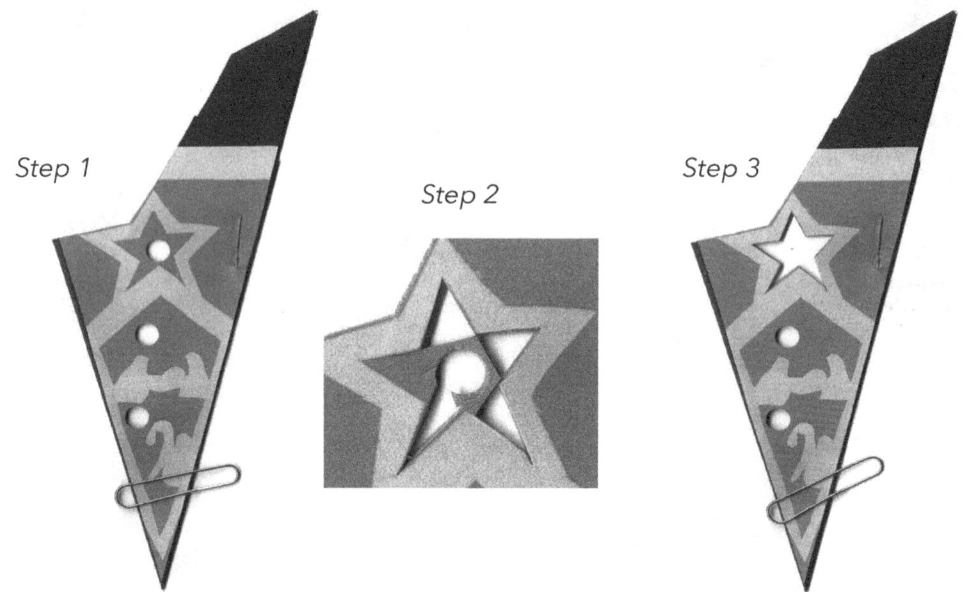

Steps 4-9: Use a small pair of sharp tipped scissors to expand the hole made by the hole punch. Divide the shaded area into multiple pieces to make removal easier.

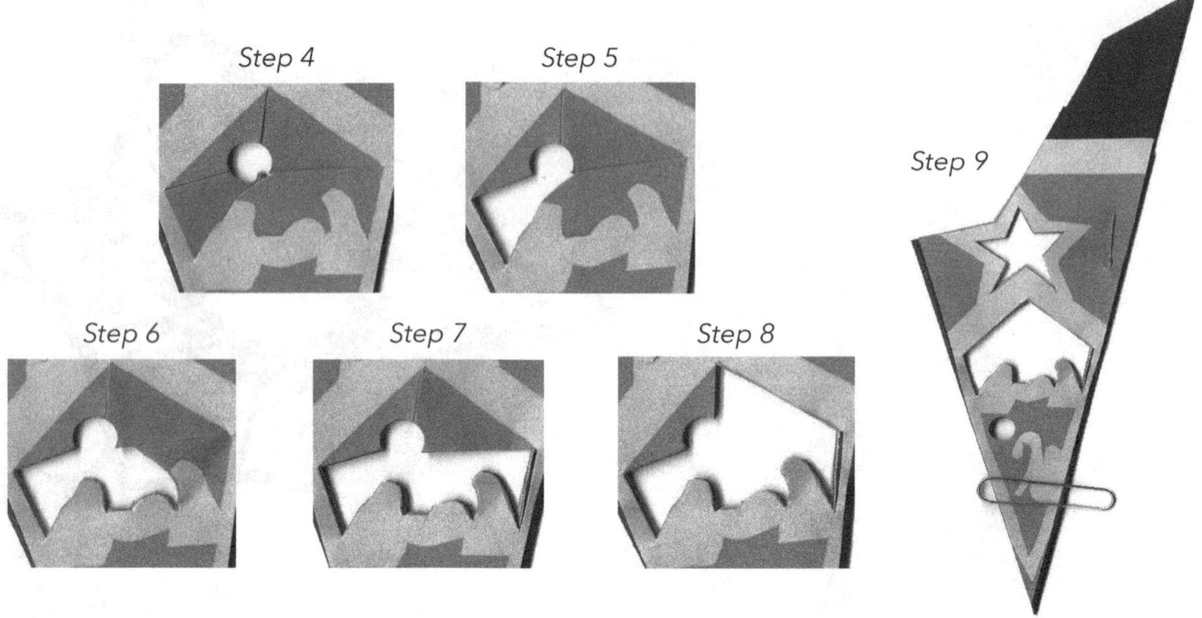

Steps 10–14: Expand the opening using a small pair of sharp tipped scissors. Continue working a little at a time until you have removed the shaded area of the pattern.

Step 10 *Step 11* *Step 12* *Step 13*

Step 14

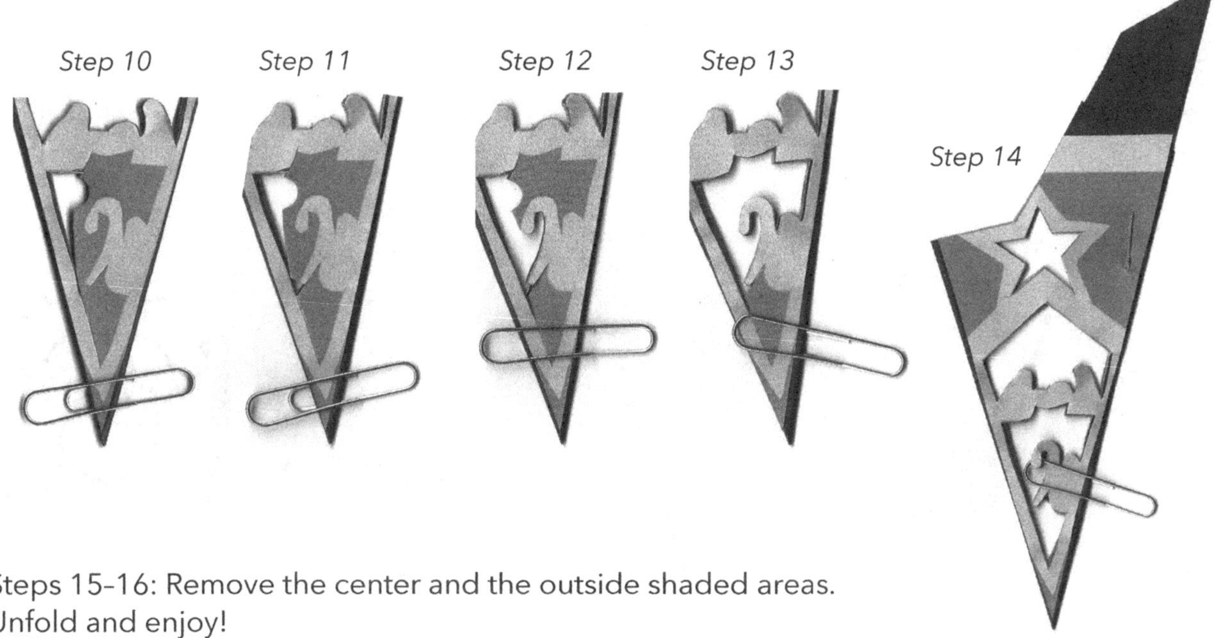

Steps 15–16: Remove the center and the outside shaded areas. Unfold and enjoy!

Step 15

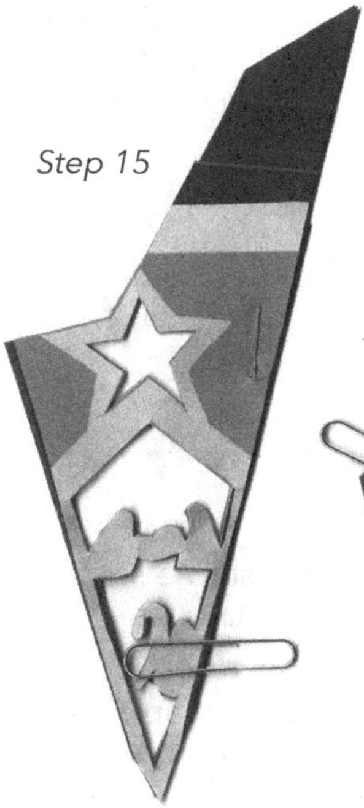

Step 16

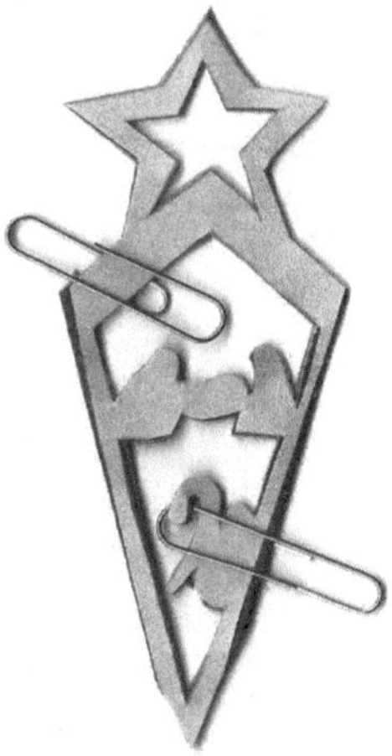

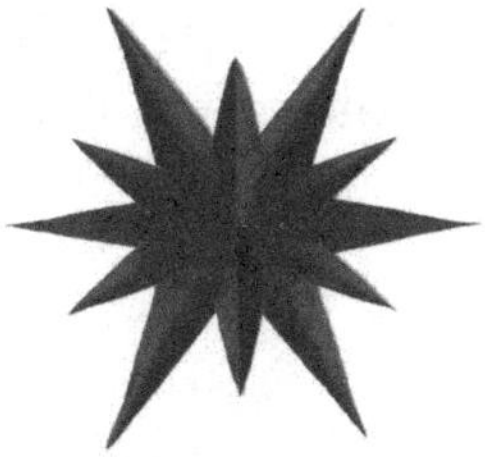

Unfold and enjoy!

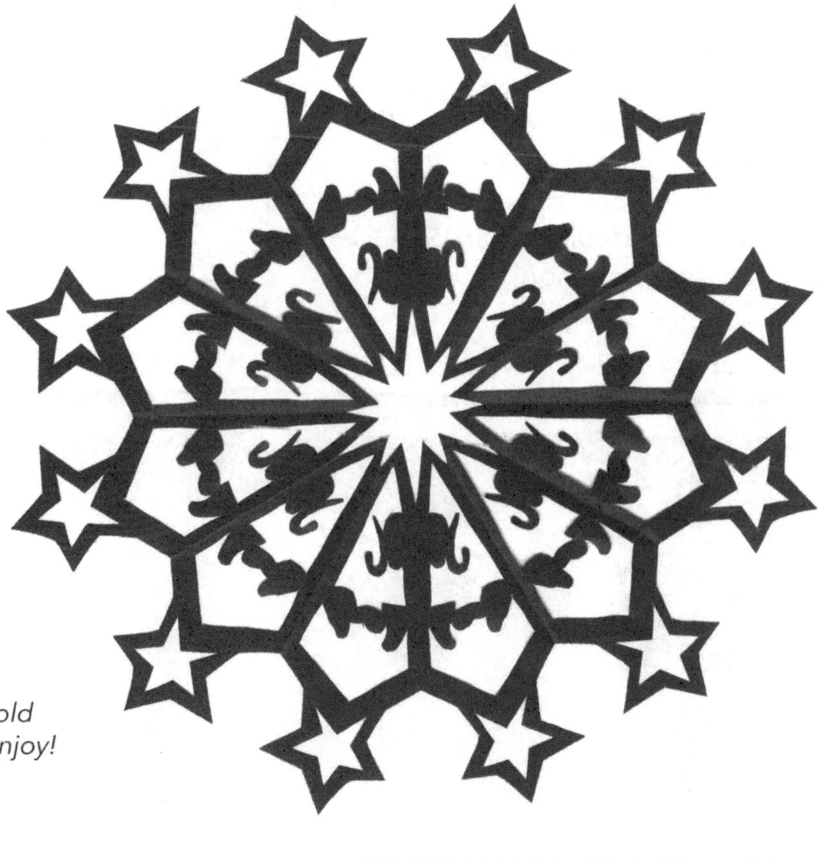

HUMBLE BIRTH 2

**See pattern on page 89.*

Follow along with the steps and their corresponding images below.

Steps 1–3: A sheep's face can be made with a series of punches. The black circles show how the punches overlap.

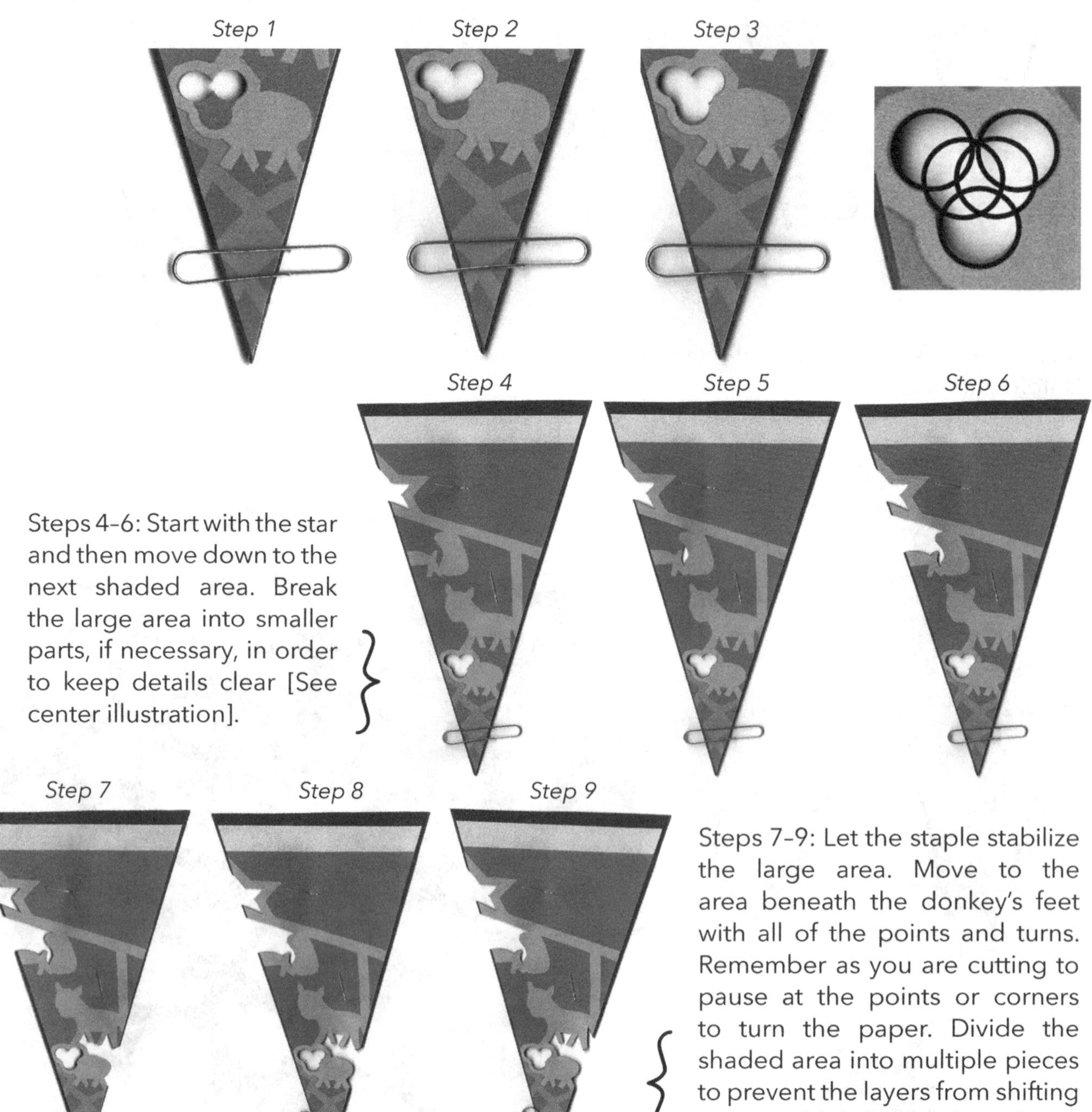

Steps 4–6: Start with the star and then move down to the next shaded area. Break the large area into smaller parts, if necessary, in order to keep details clear [See center illustration].

Steps 7-9: Let the staple stabilize the large area. Move to the area beneath the donkey's feet with all of the points and turns. Remember as you are cutting to pause at the points or corners to turn the paper. Divide the shaded area into multiple pieces to prevent the layers from shifting apart and for easier removal.

Steps 10–14: Continue to remove the shaded areas, leaving the stapled areas until the end for stability. Unfold and enjoy!

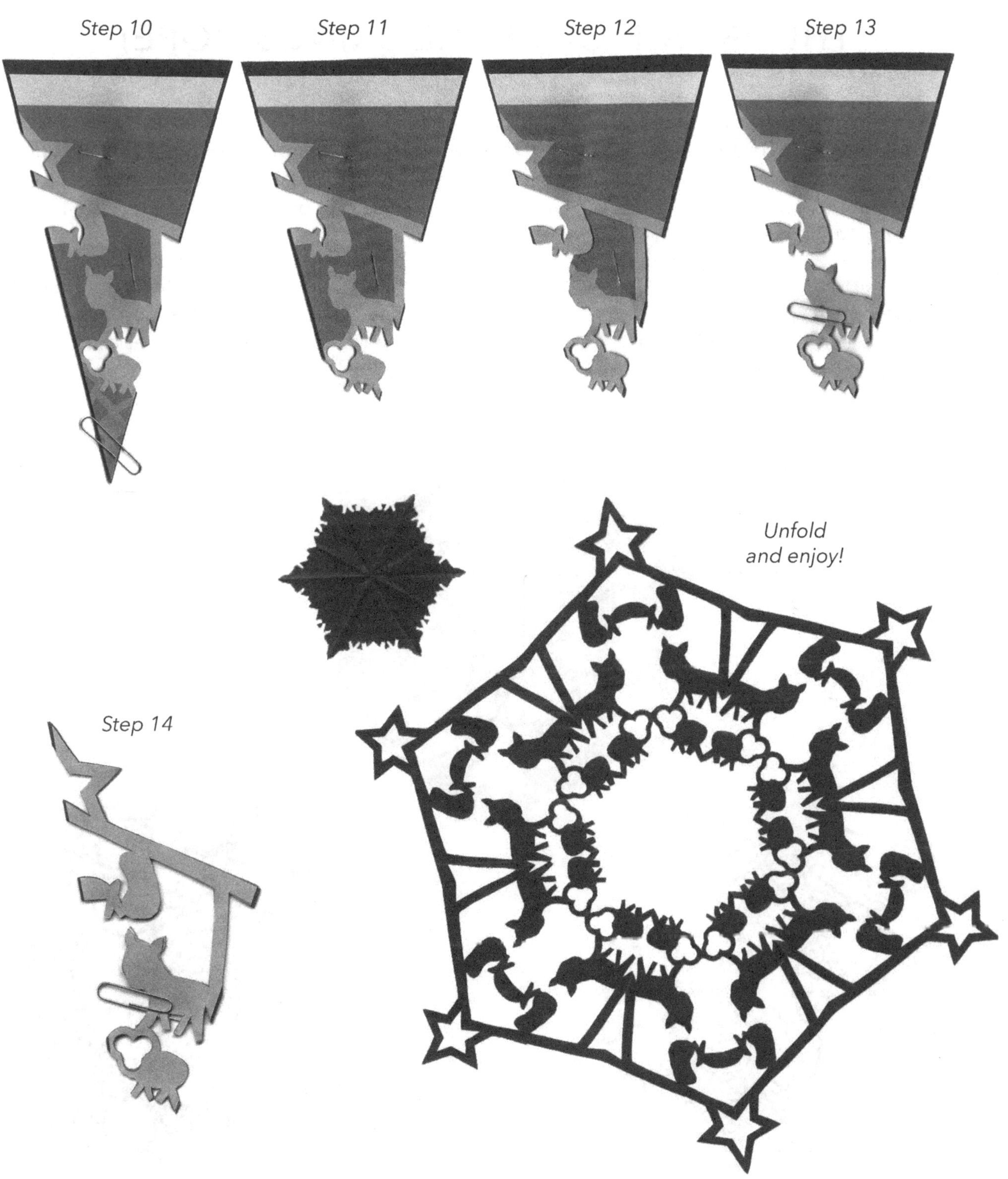

Cutting Snowflakes

THE PRINCE OF PEACE BRINGS HOPE!

OUR HEAVENLY FATHER SENT HIS SON, JESUS CHRIST, as a fulfillment of prophecy and as our only hope to return to be with Him. Despite our imperfections, we know that through Christ we can be saved! This hope gives us peace even in the midst of sorrow and pain. Hope comforts us and increases our desire to improve ourselves and our circumstances [See Isaiah 9:6, John 14:27, 16:33, and Philippians 4:7].

Center Page: A lot of symbolism is included in the Symbol Snowflake: the star, the manger, and the donkey. If you look closely, you will notice that the space between the donkeys' faces is reminiscent of a dove in flight. This Snowflake represents the humble birth of our Savior, Jesus Christ, as well as the joyous fulfillment of promises.

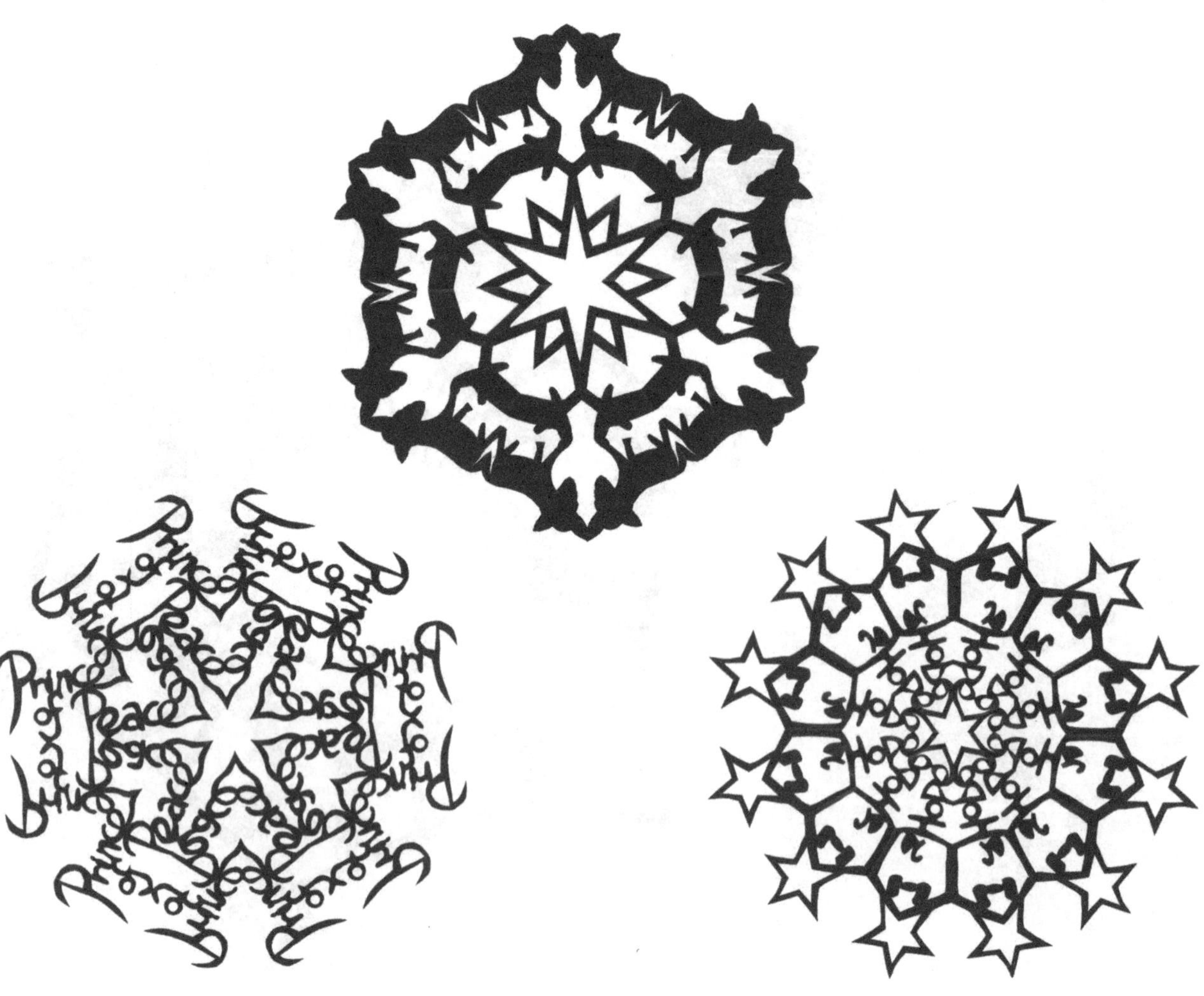

PRINCE OF PEACE

**See pattern on page 89.*

Follow along with the steps and their corresponding images below.

Steps 1–4: Remove part of the shaded area to allow the hole punch to reach the interior of the letters, if necessary. Expand the opening with a small pair of sharp tipped scissors. Continue removing the shaded areas. Staples are helpful for stabilizing the paper.

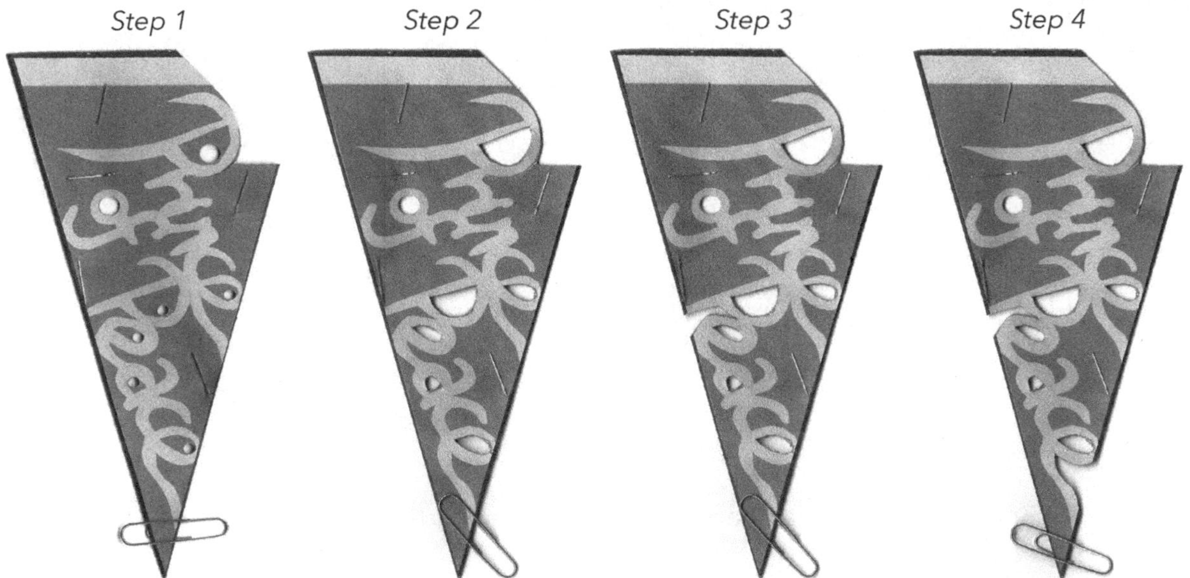

Steps 5–8: Try to do the more complicated areas first. Divide the shaded areas into smaller pieces when necessary to aid in removal. Avoid awkward positions which may cause the layers of paper to slide apart as you cut. Stabilize with paper clips as needed.

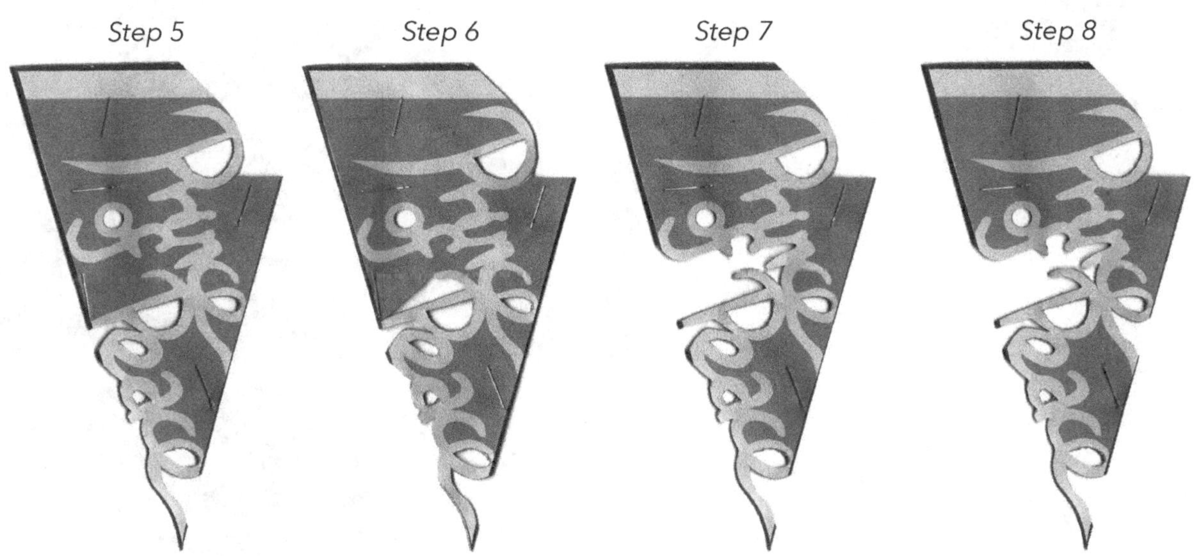

PRINCE OF PEACE (continued)

Steps 9-12: Continue removing the shaded areas. Staples and paper clips are highly recommended for holding the layers of paper together. Shifting paper can cause a lot of frustration! . . . and loss of letters.

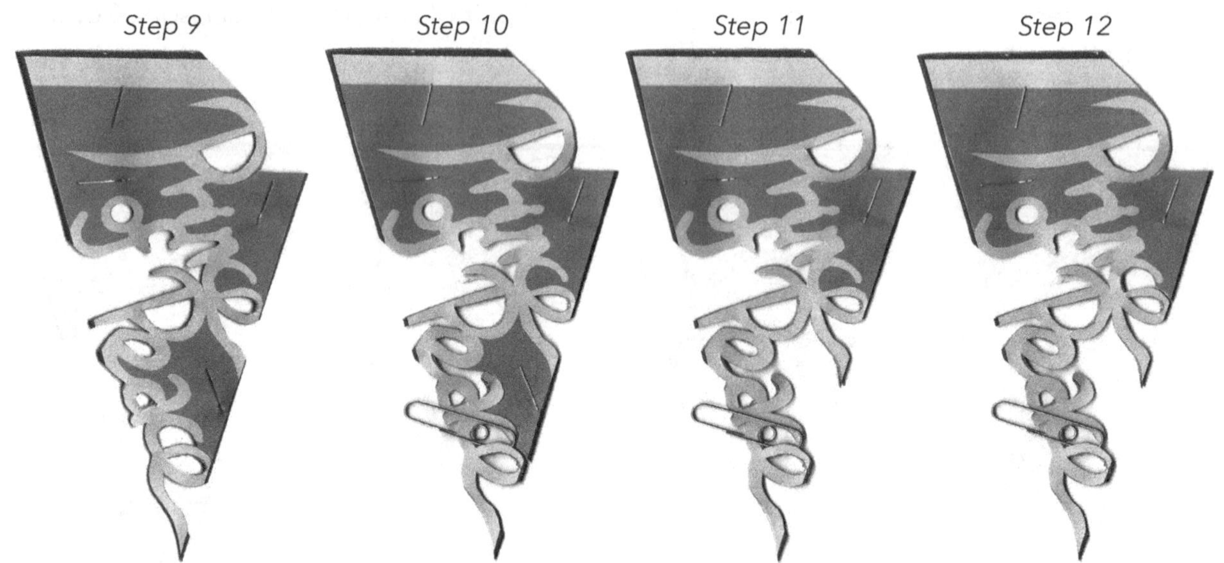

Steps 13–14: Finish removing the shaded area on the outside of the pattern. Unfold and enjoy!

SYMBOLS

See pattern on page 84.

Follow along with the steps and their corresponding images below.

Steps 1–4: Start with the more complicated area first, the one with the most points and corners. Divide the shaded area into multiple parts to prevent the layers of paper from sliding apart and to make it easier to remove. Remember to pause at the points or corners while cutting to turn the paper.

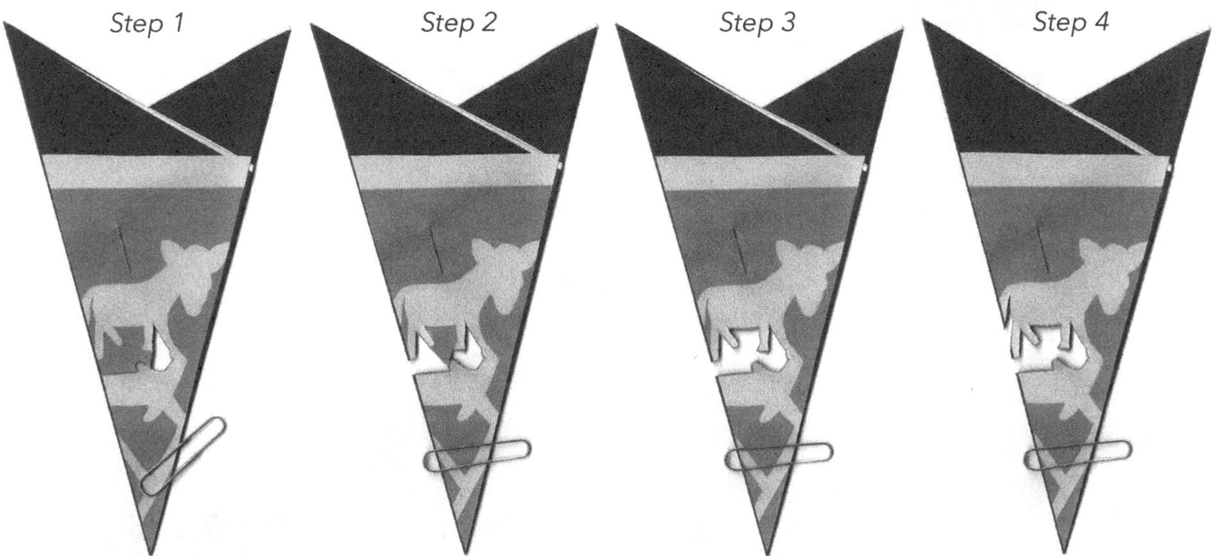

Steps 5–7: Continue cutting away the shaded areas, working toward the center. The area between the donkey's faces looks like a dove in flight.

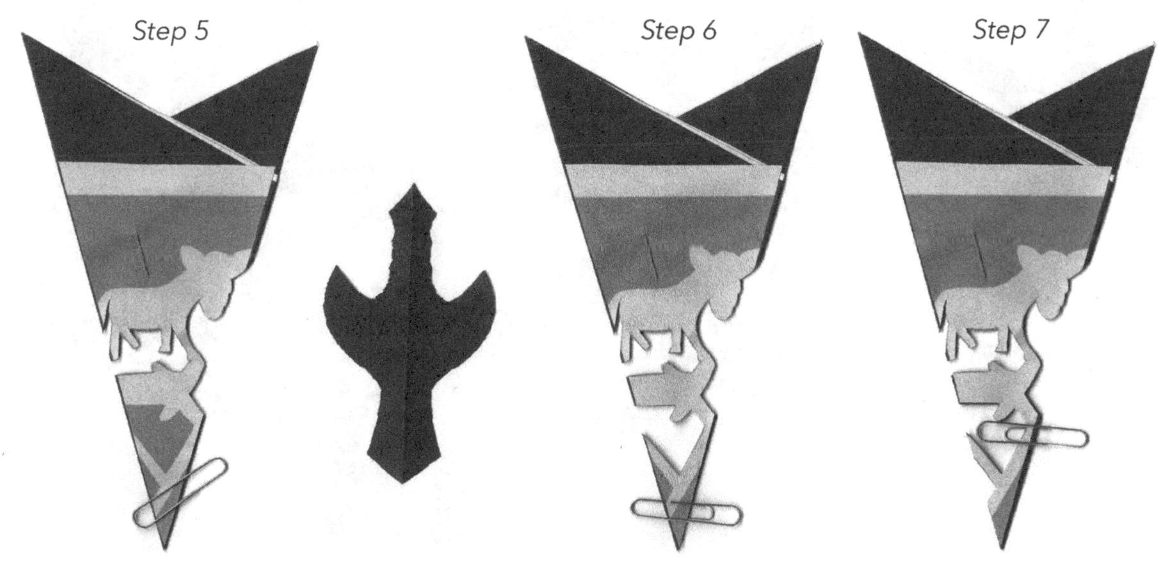

SYMBOLS (continued)

Steps 8–9: Remove the shaded area on the outside of the pattern. Unfold and enjoy!

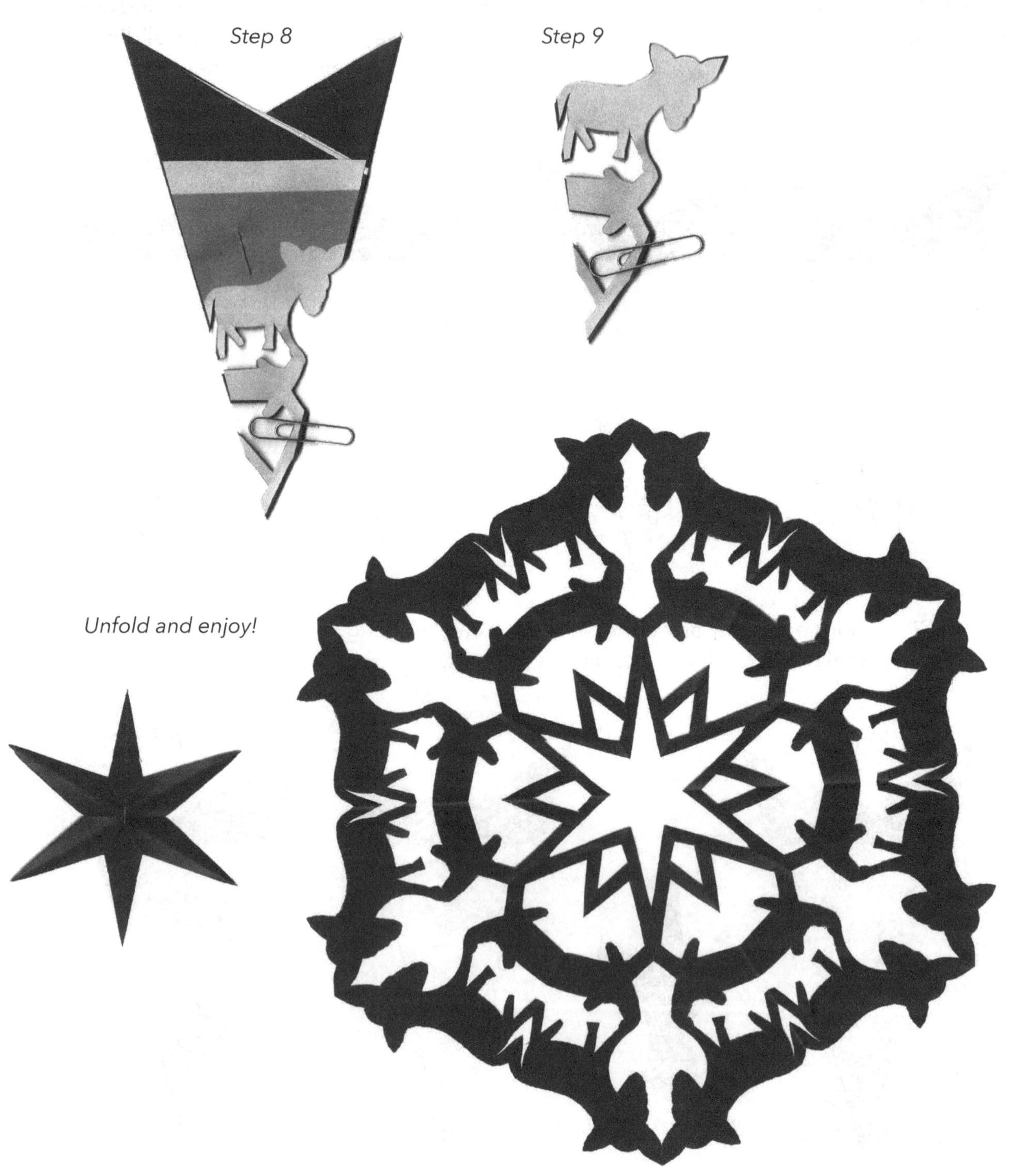

Step 8

Step 9

Unfold and enjoy!

HOPE NATIVITY

**See pattern on page 90.*

Follow along with the steps and their corresponding images below.

Steps 1-3: Remove part of the shaded area if necessary to reach the interior areas with a hole punch. Use the hole punch to create an opening and then finish the interior with a small pair of sharp tipped scissors [See Gloria on page 86 for a more detailed star].

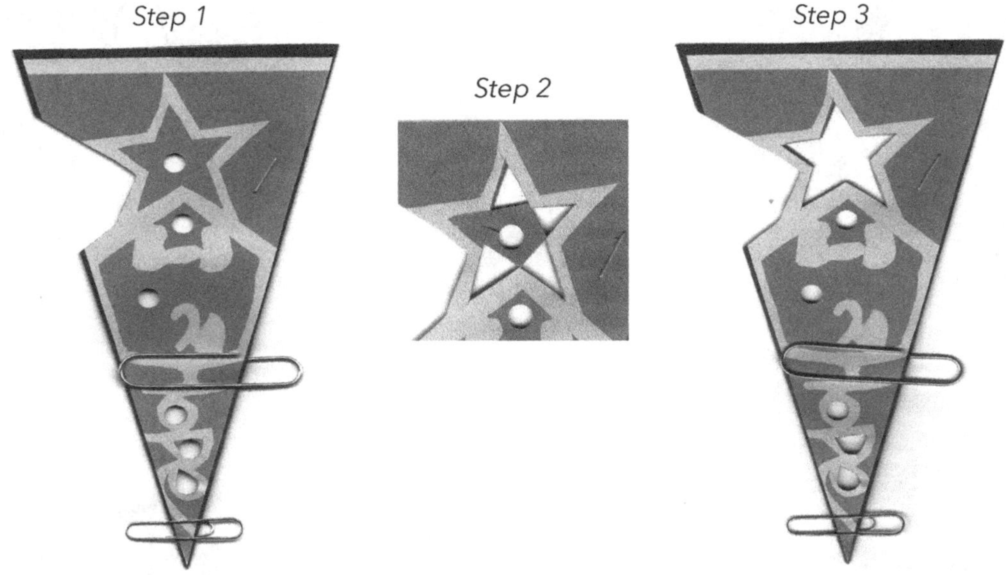

Steps 4-16: Expand the opening until you can maneuver the scissors in the area needing to be cut. Divide the shaded area into sections as needed for removal.

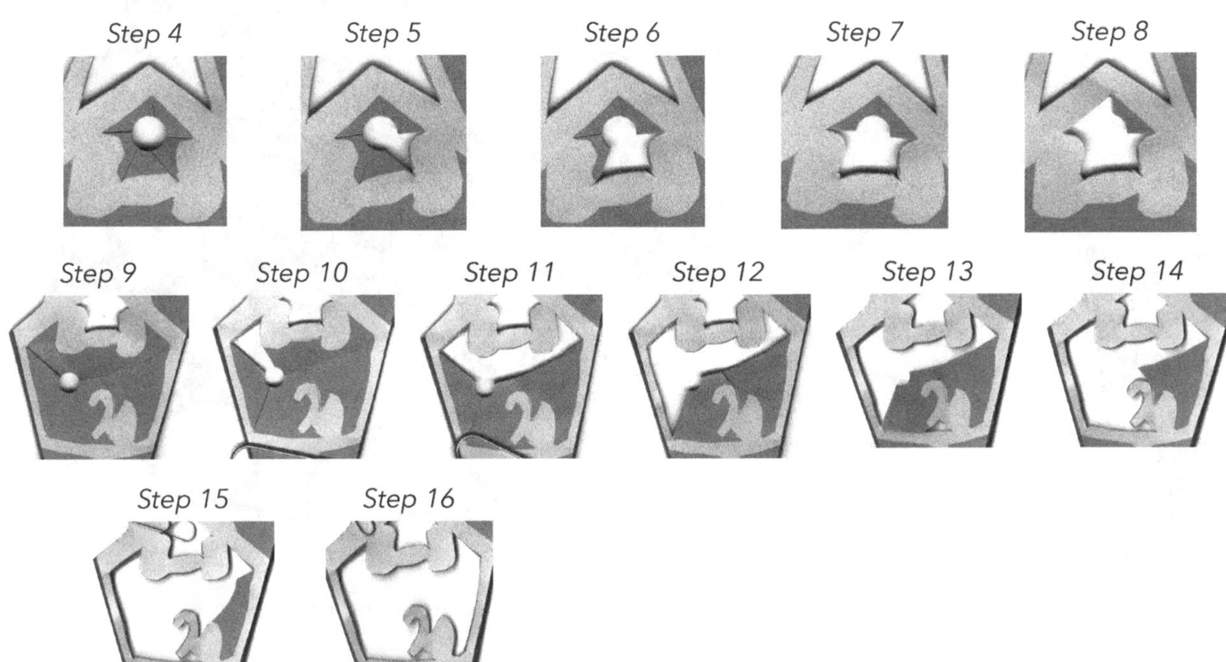

HOPE NATIVITY (continued)

Steps 17-24: Paper clips are great for stabilizing areas that have already been cut out! Continue removing shaded areas, working toward the center. To prevent the paper from shifting, divide the outer edge into sections. Unfold and enjoy!

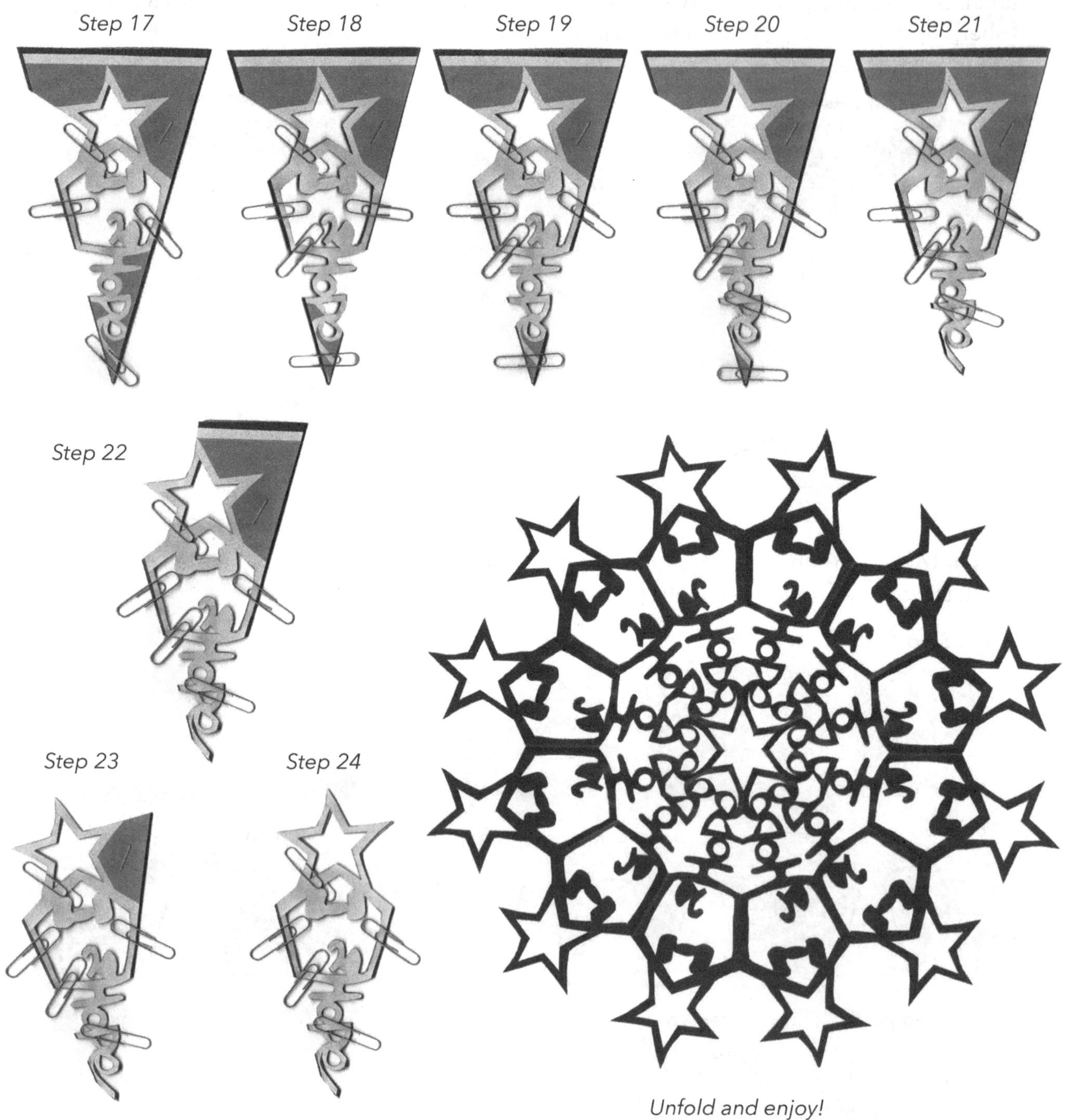

Unfold and enjoy!

BONUS PATTERN: STENCIL-LIKE NATIVITY

*See pattern on page 85.

Follow along with the steps and their corresponding images below.

Steps 1–6: Cut out the angels in this order: head, halo, wings, then body. After the shaded area of the pattern has been removed, unfold and enjoy!

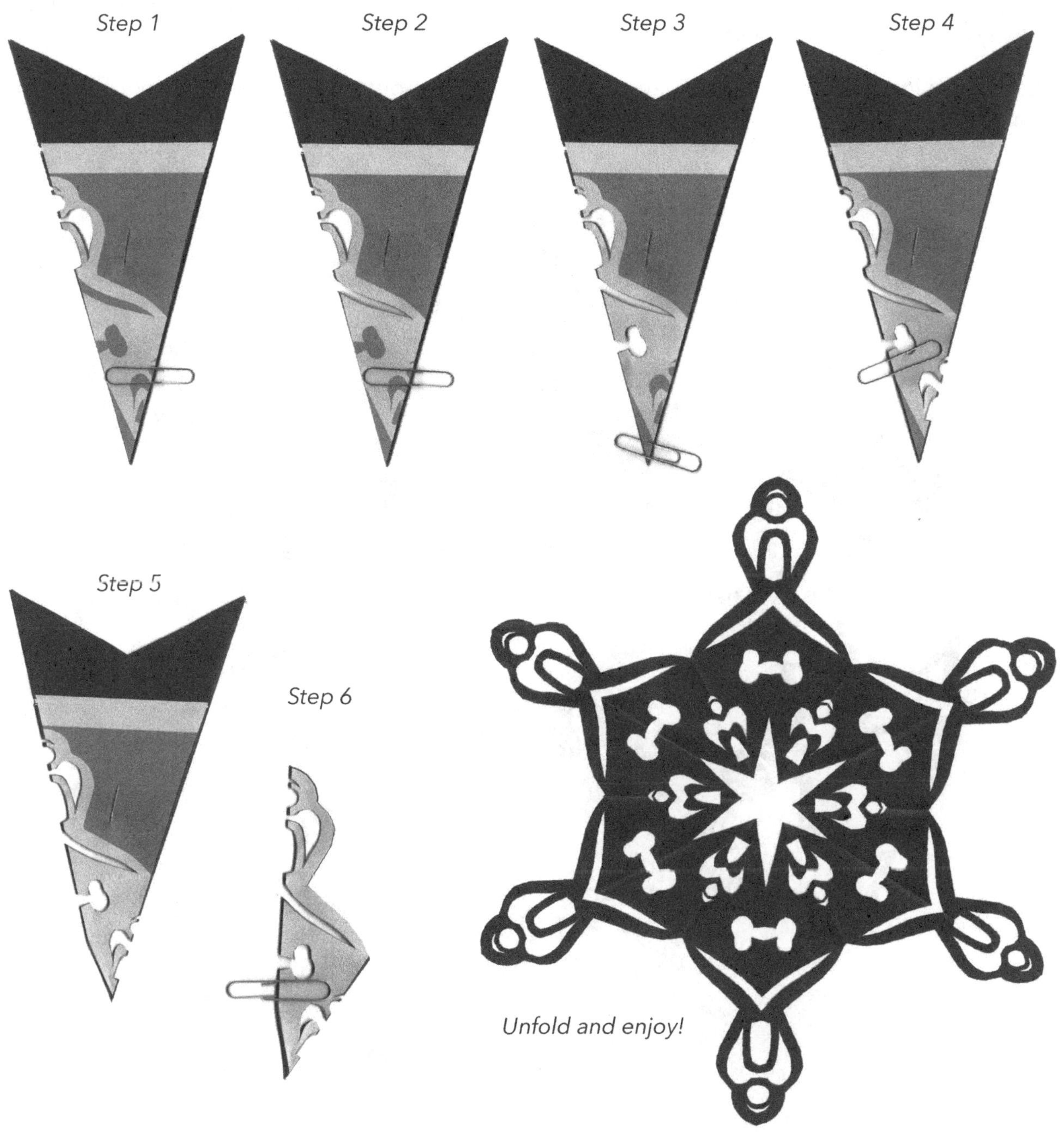

Unfold and enjoy!

Cutting Snowflakes

XL NATIVITY

THE GLORIOUS YET HUMBLE BIRTH OF OUR SAVIOR JESUS CHRIST awes us both with its majesty and humility. There was no room at the inn that Holy Night, Luke 2:7, but may there always be room in our hearts to let him in!

Let us rejoice during the Christmas season and throughout the year as we think of our Lord and Savior, Jesus Christ! Alma 26:11-16

XL NATIVITY

*See pattern on page 91.

Follow along with the steps and their corresponding images below.

Steps 1–8: Remove part of the shaded area if needed to reach the interior areas with a hole punch. Use a small pair of sharp tipped scissors to expand the opening. Divide the shaded area as needed for removal [see Gloria on page 33 for more pictures of a star].

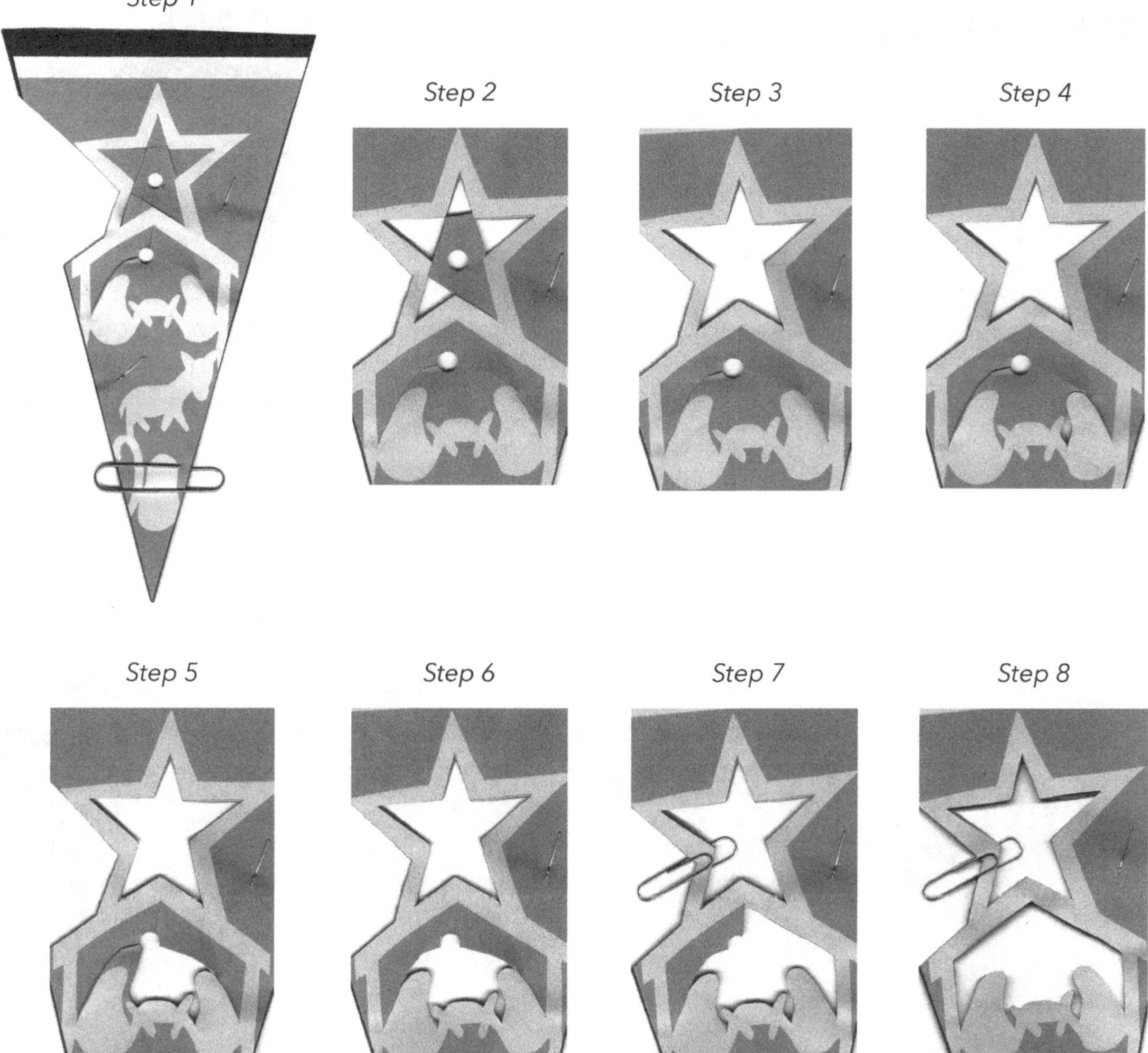

XL NATIVITY (continued)

Steps 9–14: Allow the staple to stabilize the large central area. Move to the area beneath the donkey's feet with lots of opportunities to practice pausing while cutting to turn the paper. Challenge yourself to cut the area out as one piece or break the area into multiple pieces for easier removal. Be mindful of the layers of paper and stabilize with paper clips if you feel them sliding apart.

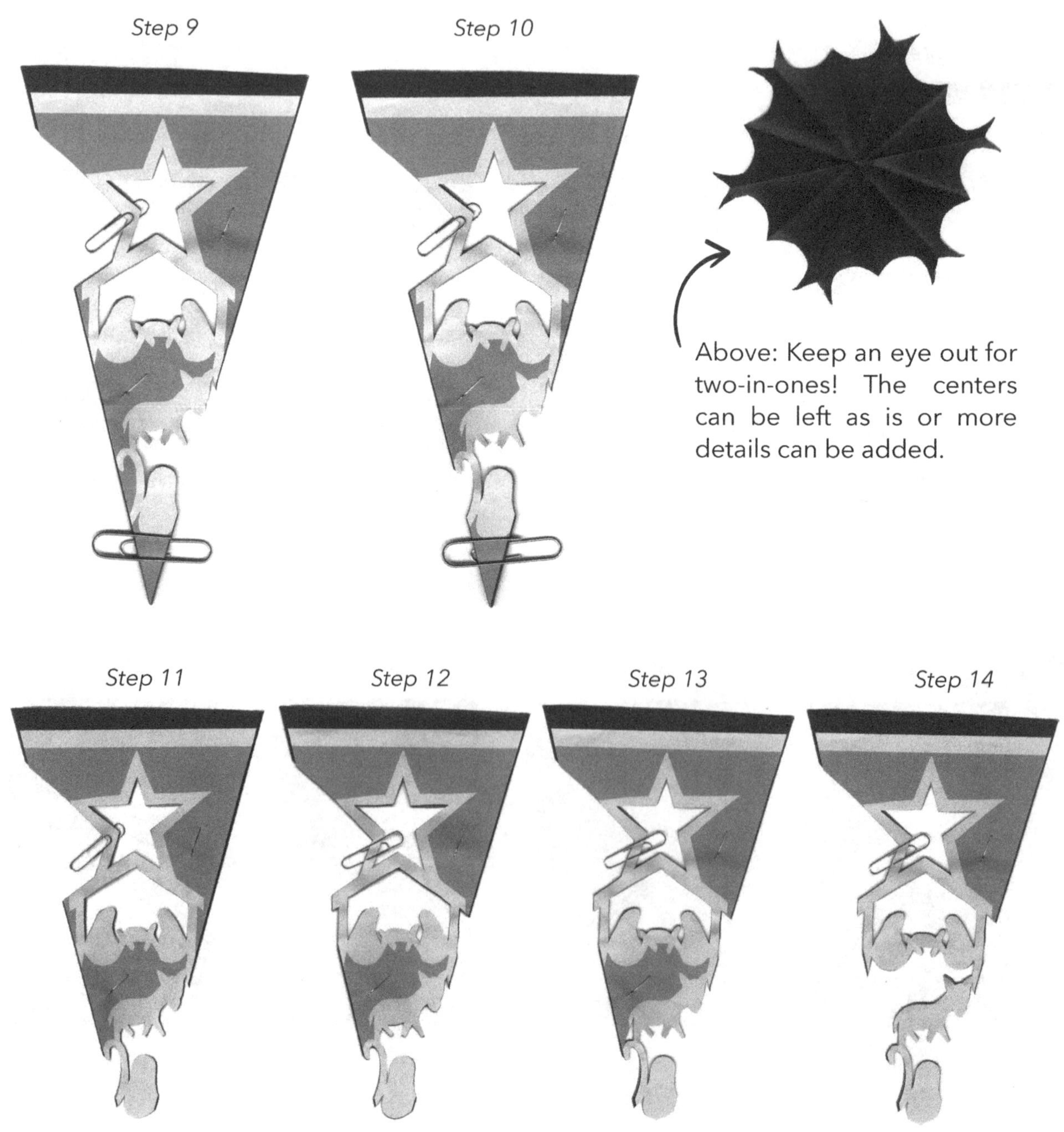

Above: Keep an eye out for two-in-ones! The centers can be left as is or more details can be added.

Steps 15–17: Remove the shaded area from the outside of the pattern. Use paper clips to divide the shaded area into sections to prevent the paper from shifting. Unfold and enjoy!

Unfold and enjoy!

Cutting Snowflakes

JOY TO THE WORLD

LIKE THE ANGELS OF OLD, we want to proclaim to the world the great joy that we feel when we come to know our Savior, Jesus Christ [Luke 2:10-11, Galatians 5:22, Alma 19:6]!

Whether your testimony is expressed through word, music, visual arts, or service, I hope that you will be able to share your love of Christ with others this Christmas season!

Below: This snowflake can be cut out in more than one way. The example below shows an alternative way of cutting out the interior space. It is challenging! . . . but results in a more stable snowflake (more connections). The directions on the following pages use access cuts instead to remove the shaded area around the words 'to' and 'the.'

TIP: Interior spaces can be further divided to make them less challenging.

JOY TO THE WORLD

See pattern on page 90.

Follow along with the steps and their corresponding images below.

Step 1: Attach pattern to folded paper and use hole punch for the interior of the letters.

Step 2: Use a small pair of scissors to finish cutting out the 'e' and the large 'O.'

Step 3: Cut out the more complicated shaded area on the upper right.

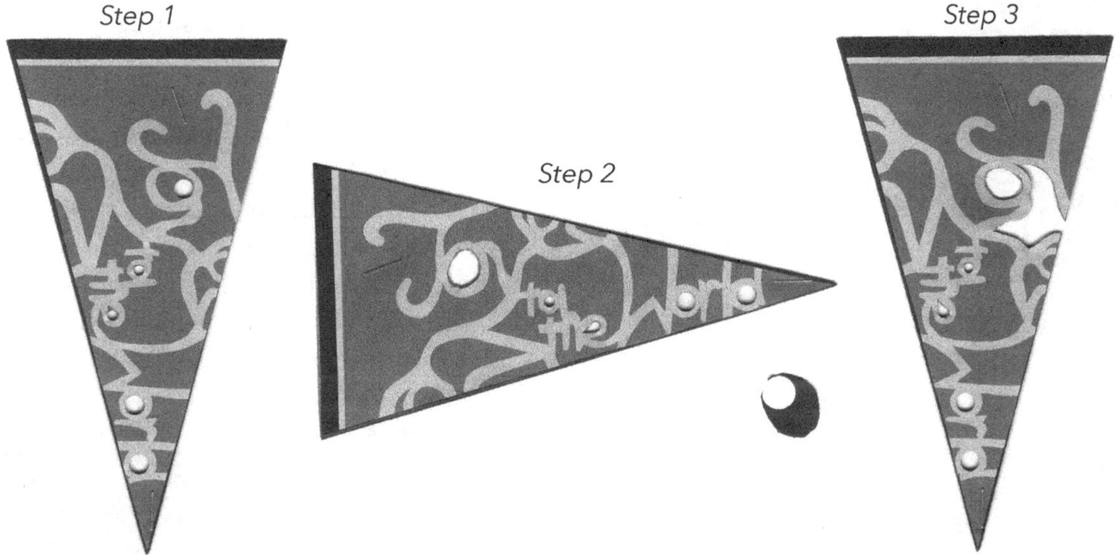

Steps 4-7: Cut out the top angel. Remember when cutting out the face to start with the scissors perpendicular to the edge of the paper to avoid pointy heads. Check the cut-out shape to make sure it is to your liking before proceeding [See far left].

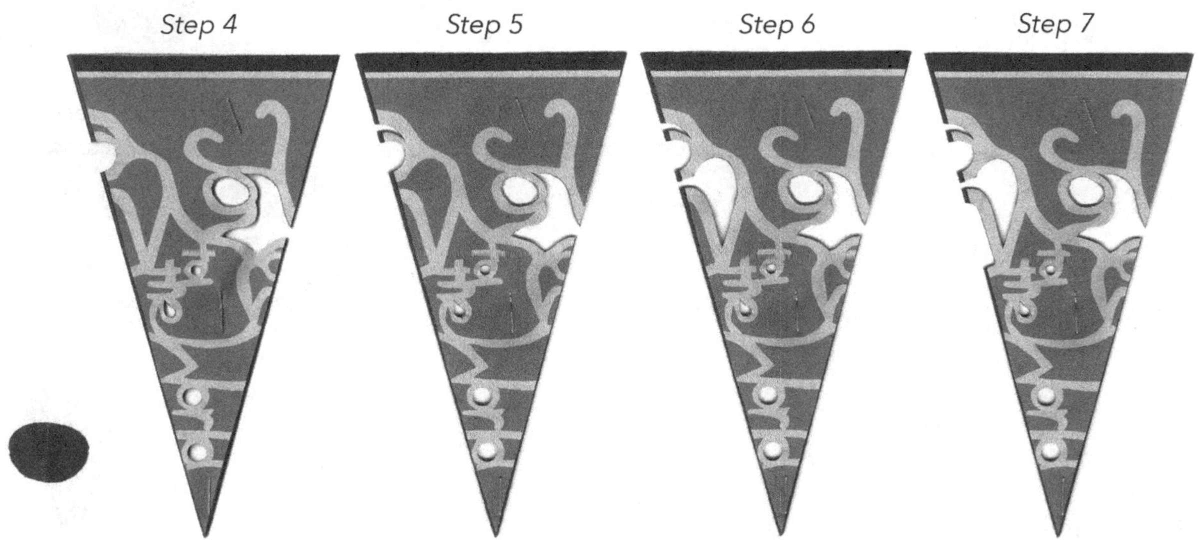

JOY TO THE WORLD (continued)

Step 8: Create an access cut and cut away the area between the 't' and 'h' in the word 'the.' Note: the access cut goes all the way to the asterisk.

Step 9: Finish cutting out the area beneath the word 'the.'

Step 8

ACCESS CUT

Step 9

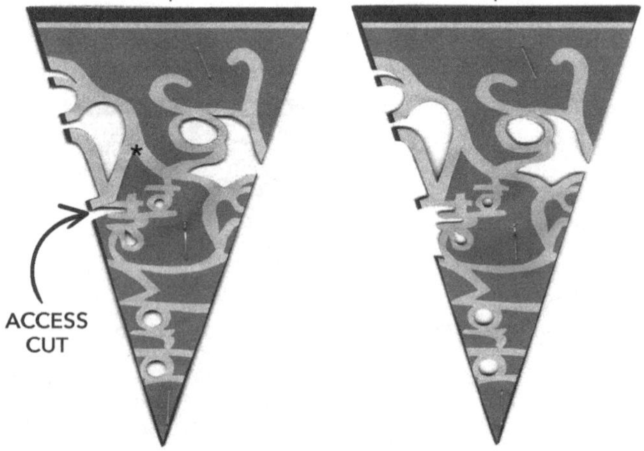

Steps 10–13: From the access cut previously made, make a series of additional cuts (more or less, as needed) in order to maneuver a small pair of scissors within the area to make the final cuts. Take your time and be especially careful around the 't' on the word 'to.' It is the only connection that the words 'to the' will have to the rest of the snowflake using this cutting method, see circled area below.

Step 10

Step 11

Step 12

Step 13

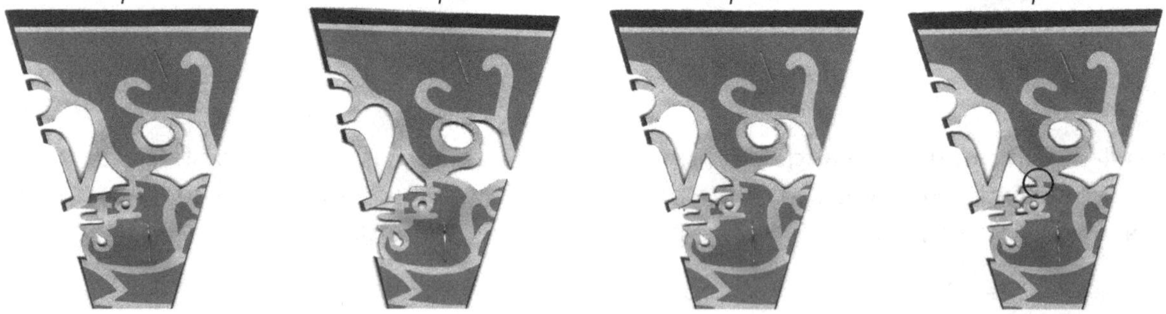

Step 14: Cut out the smaller angel [See steps used for the larger angel on the previous page].

Steps 15–16: Use an access cut between the 'e' and the 'W' and ending at the asterisk. Divide the space to remove the shaded portion from the letter 'e.' Cut along the more challenging area first (dividing again, as needed) to remove the remaining shaded area.

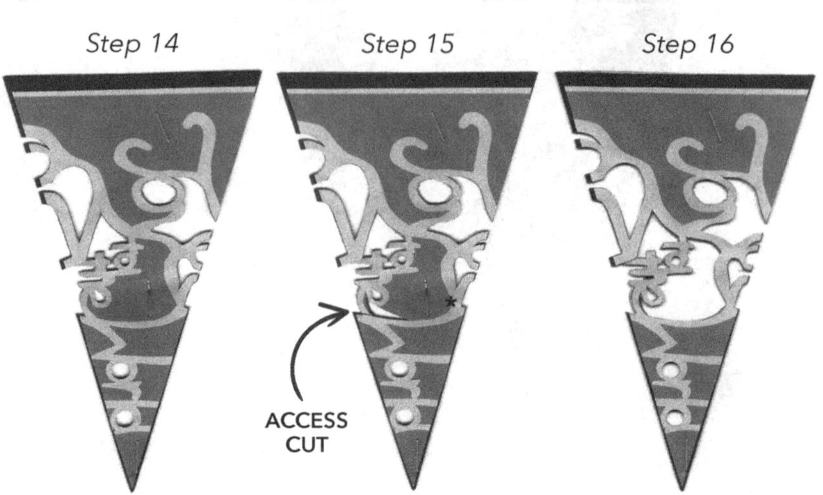

Steps 17–21: Continue cutting away the shaded area from the outside of the snowflake toward the center (leaving the outside edge until the end).

Step 17 *Step 18* *Step 19* *Step 20* *Step 21*

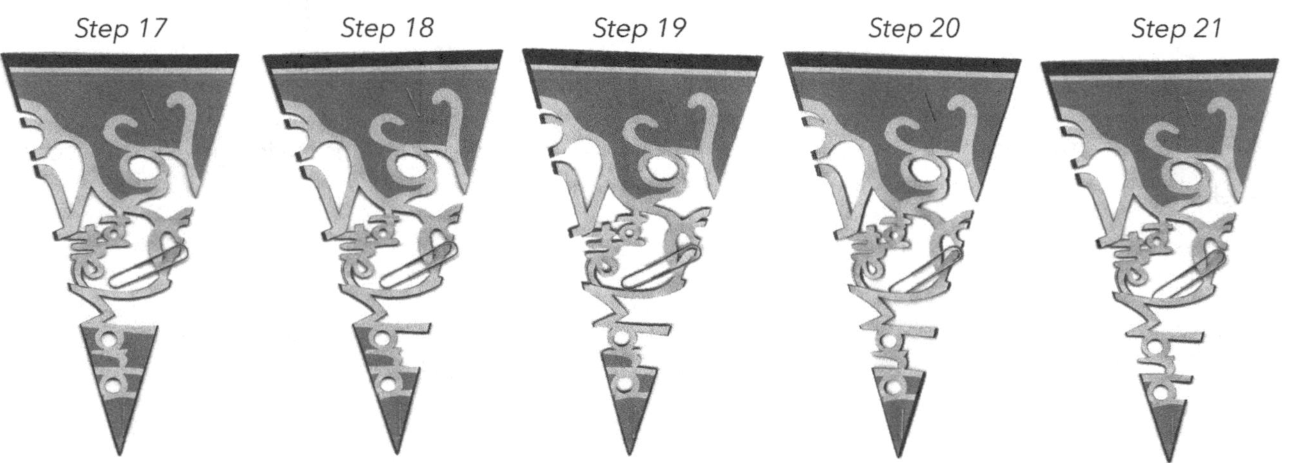

Steps 22–23: Don't forget the tiny triangle under the 'd.'

Step 22 *Step 23*

Unfold and enjoy!

Steps 24–25: Divide the remaining space into parts for ease of removal. Unfold and enjoy!

Step 24 *Step 25*

Pattern Pages and Templates

**Patterns can be copied for personal use.*

Noted beneath each pattern is the size of the square of paper that it is designed for. Use a slightly larger paper to allow room for your creativity!

TIPS:

- The shaded areas of the patterns are meant to be cut away.
- The word fold is used to mark a folded area that needs to be left intact.
- If there are two snowflakes in the same pattern, the word divide is used to show the division between the two snowflakes.
- Remember to unfold the snowflakes carefully!

See page 6 or the QR Code below for instructions on how to use the Box Folding Templates on the following pages. The Box Folding Templates are designed to be printed on 20 lb. copy paper. Each template has a QR code linked to a free pdf to make printing easier.

SCAN TO VIEW:
Box Folding Template
Quick Video

VARIEGATED BOX FOLDING TEMPLATE

**See folding instructions on page 6.*

Cut

Cut

1

2

3

4

Cut

Cut

SCAN TO VIEW:
Variegated Gray Box
Folding Template

BOX FOLDING TEMPLATE

*See folding instructions on page 6.

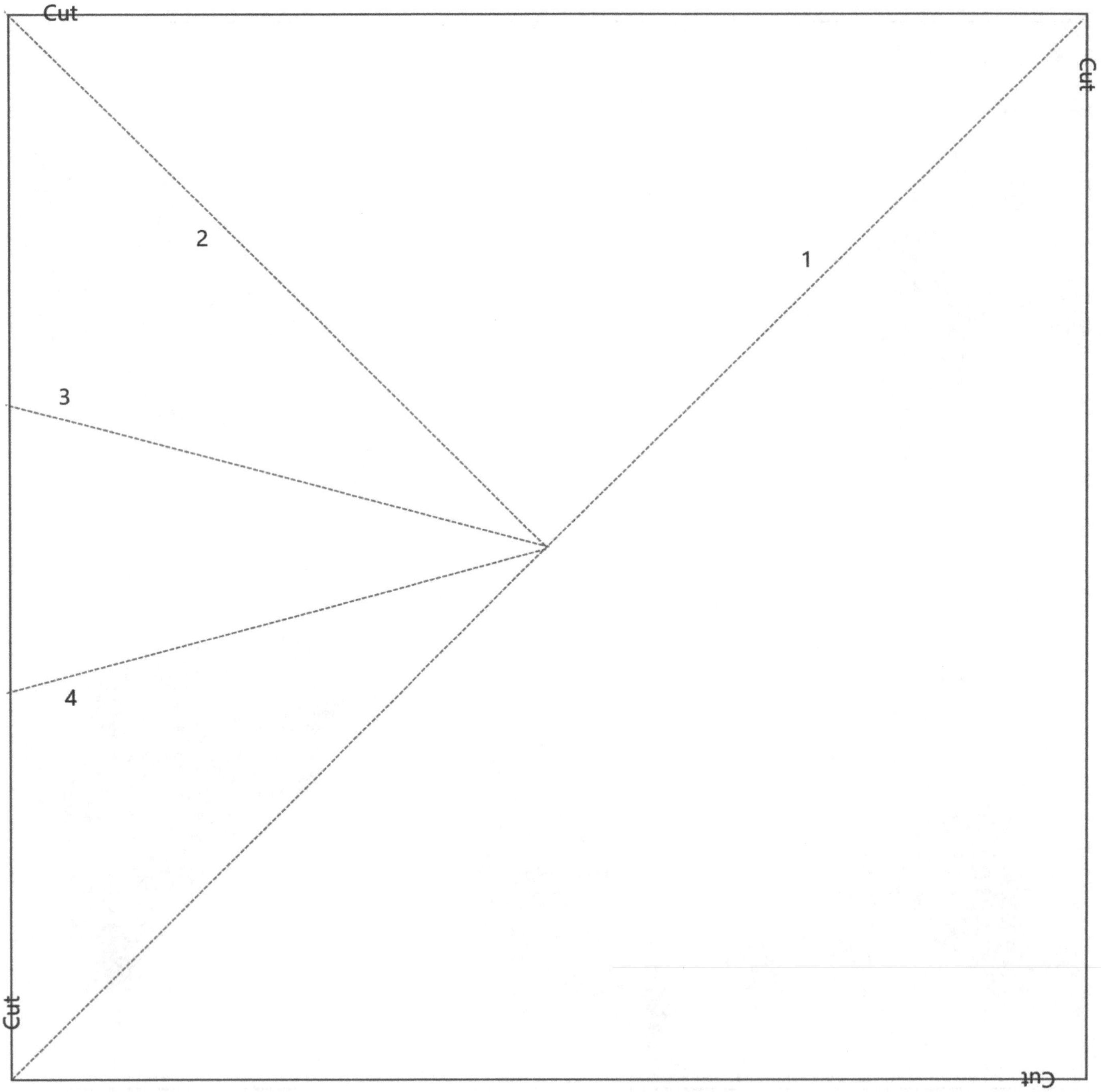

Cut

Cut

2

1

3

4

Cut

Cut

SCAN TO VIEW:
Blank Box
Folding Template

BOX FOLDING TEMPLATE: CANDLELIGHT

*See folding instructions on page 6.

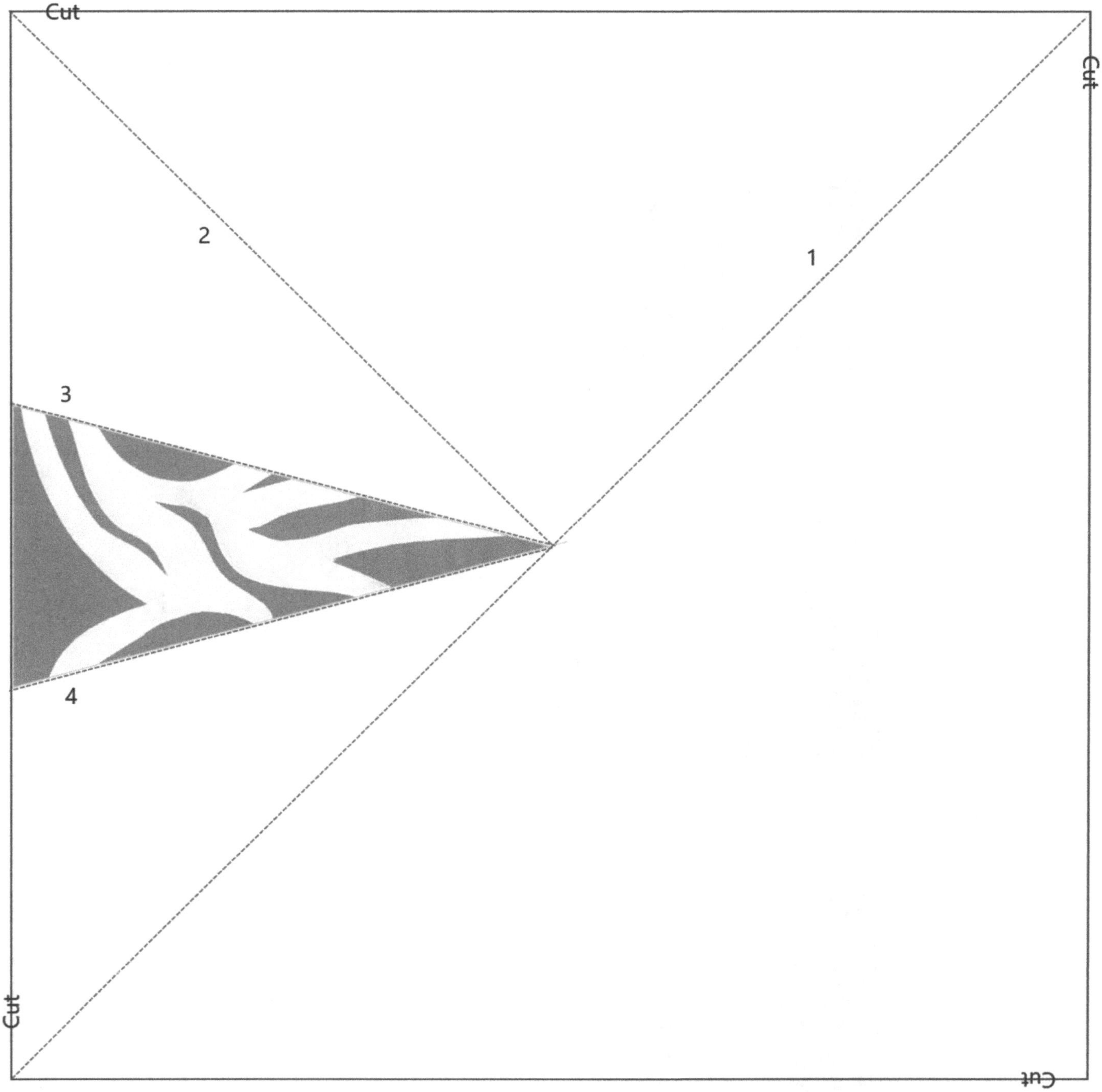

Cut

Cut

2

1

3

4

Cut

Cut

SCAN TO VIEW:
Candlelight on Box
Folding Template

EVERGREEN TREES, SNOWMEN WITH DOVES, AND SHOOTING STARS

**Designed for a 8.5″ Square of Paper.*

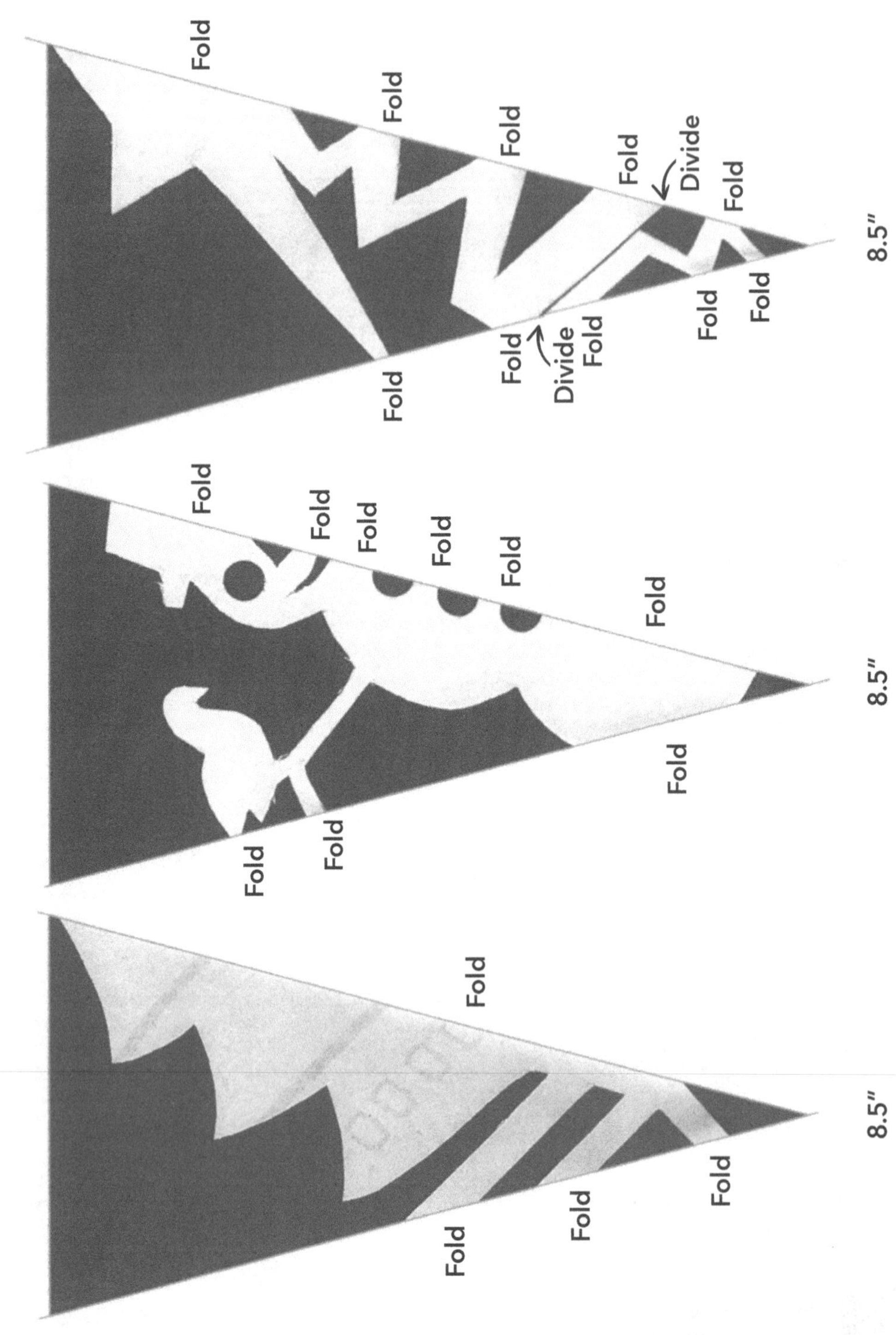

HANDBELLS, BELL TOWER, HEARTS, AND DIAMONDS

**Designed for a 8.5″ Square of Paper.*

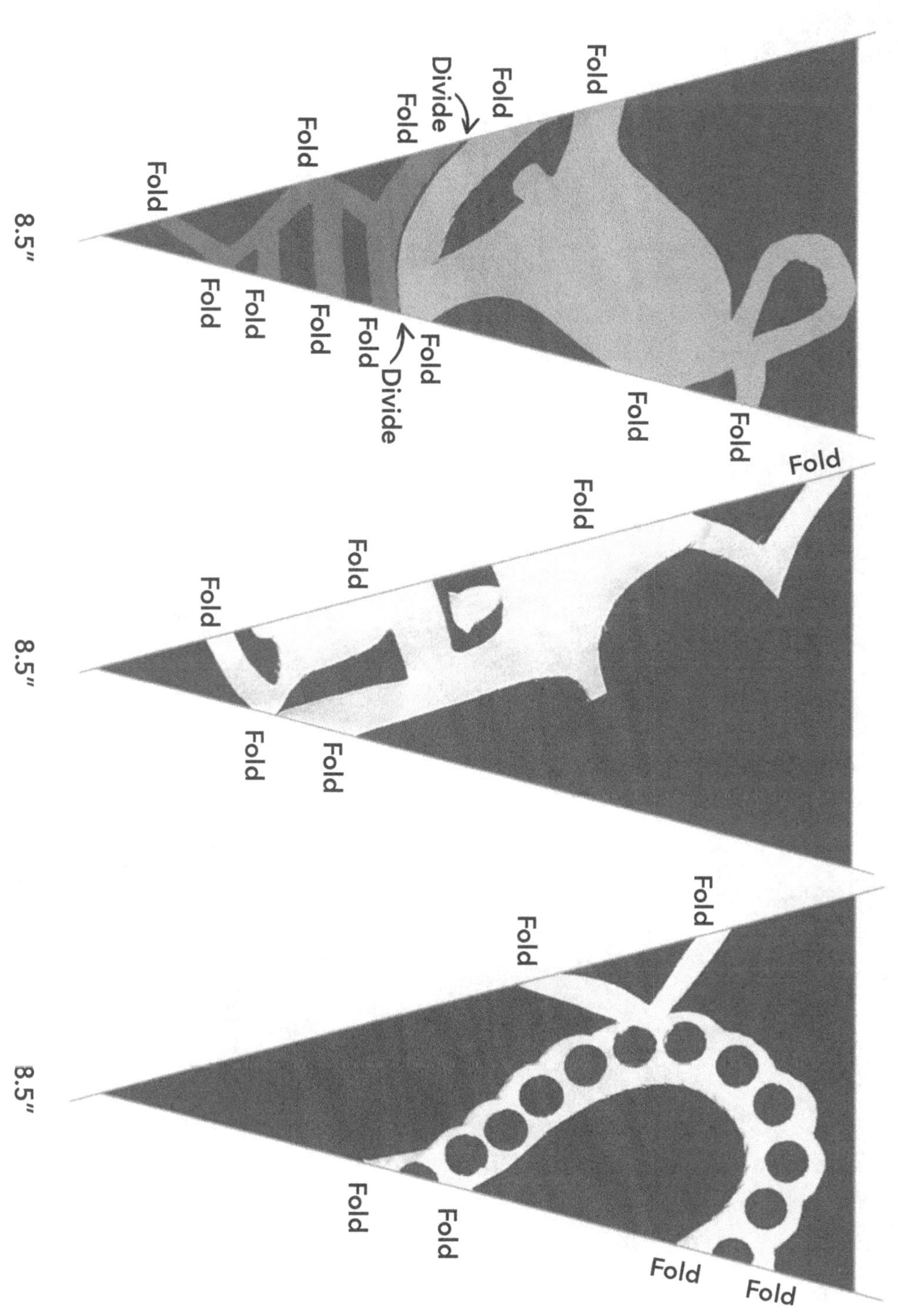

PEACE, LOVE, AND CHOIR

**Designed for a 8.5″ Square of Paper.*

BOWTIES AND BELLS, HANDBELL CHOIR, AND DADDY DAUGHTER DANCE

**Designed for a 8.5″ Square of Paper.*

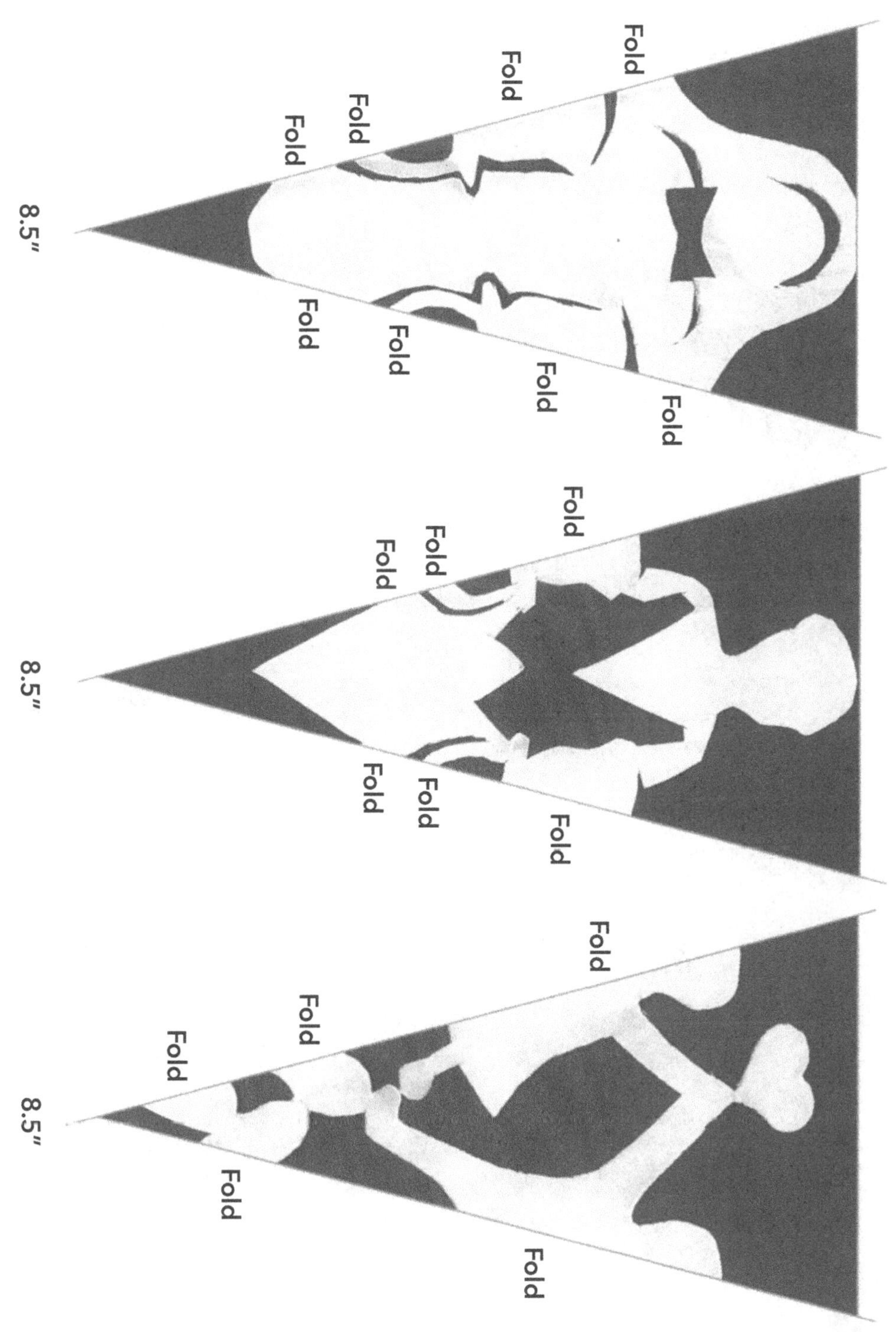

HOLDING HANDS, HUMBLE BIRTH: INTERIOR PRACTICE, AND SYMBOLS

**Designed for a 8.5″ Square of Paper.*

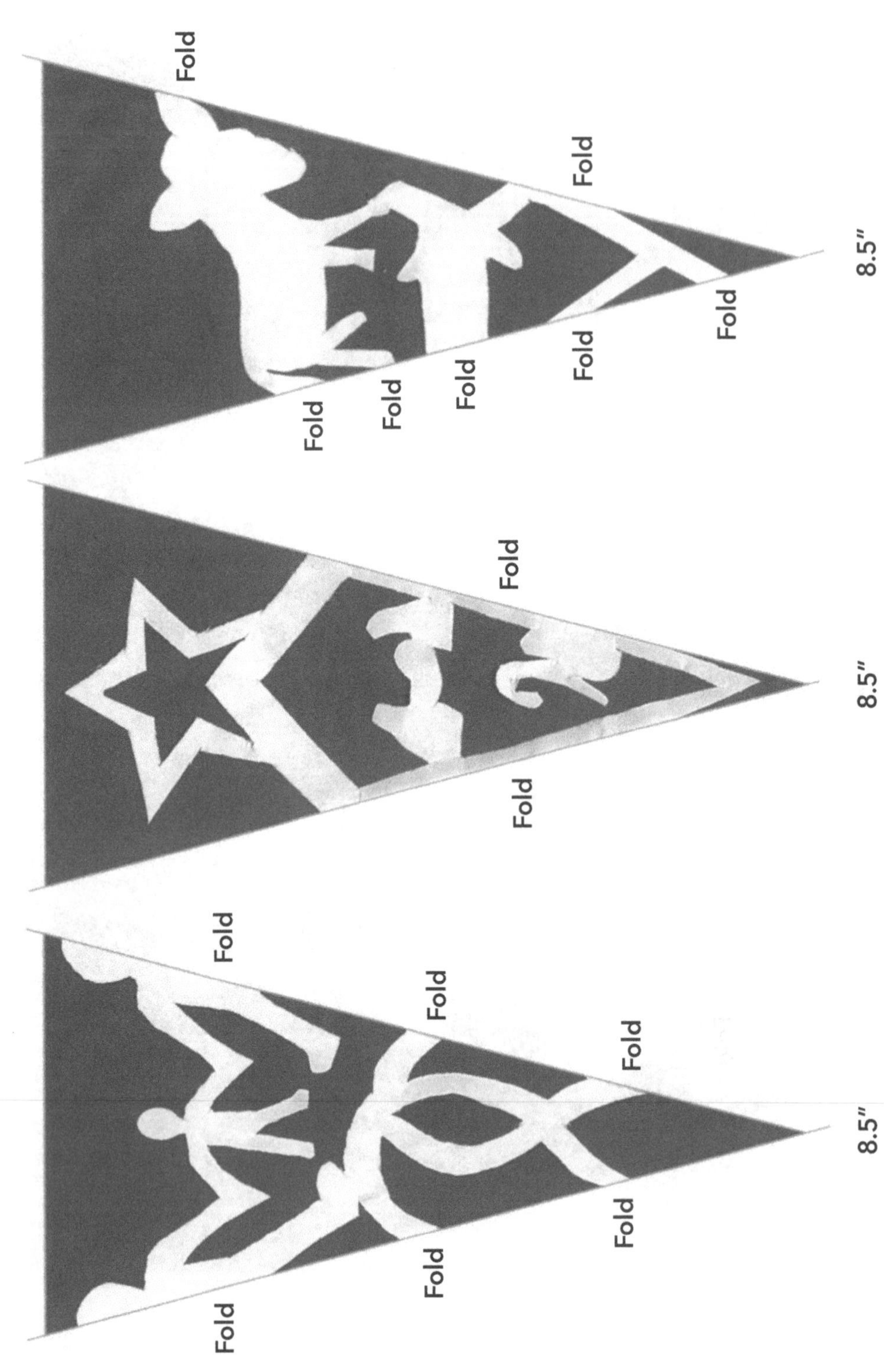

DONKEY, STENCIL-LIKE NATIVITY, AND REJOICE

**Designed for a 8.5" Square of Paper.*

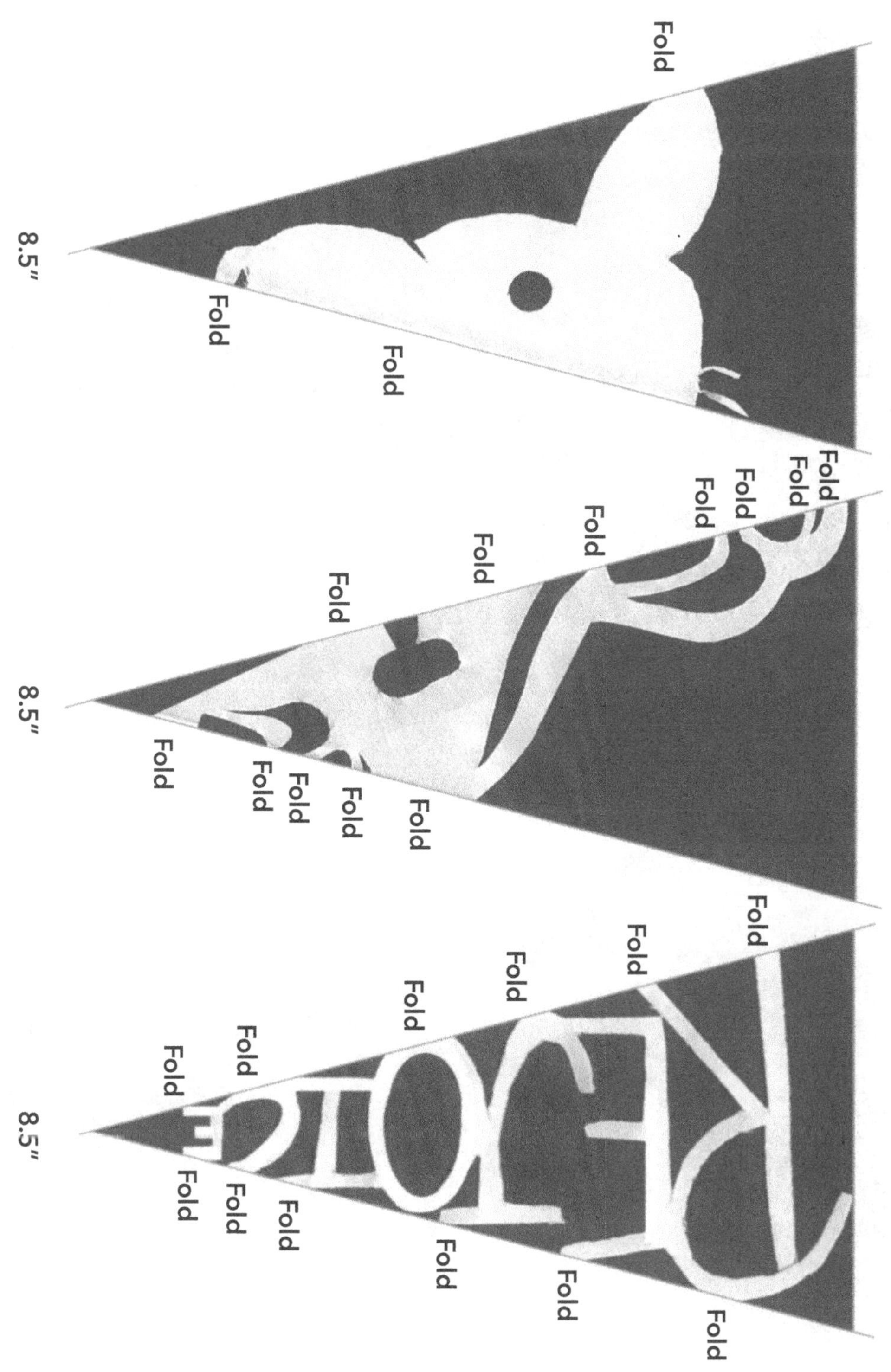

BELL TOWER WITH NOEL AND GLORIA

**Designed for a 12″ Square of Paper.*

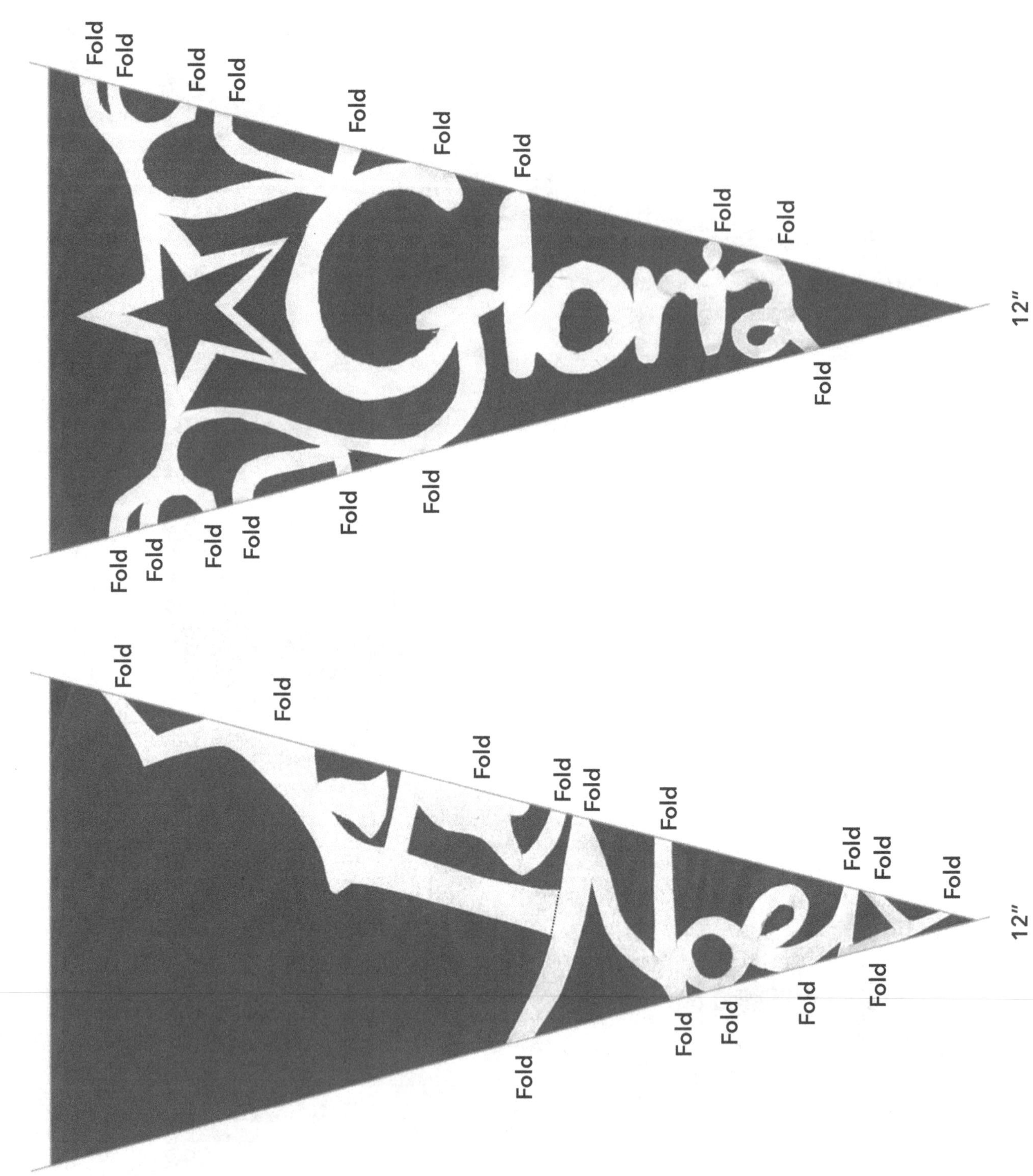

CHOIR WITH BELL TOWER AND HANDBELL
CHOIR WITH BELL TOWER

**Designed for a 12" Square of Paper.*

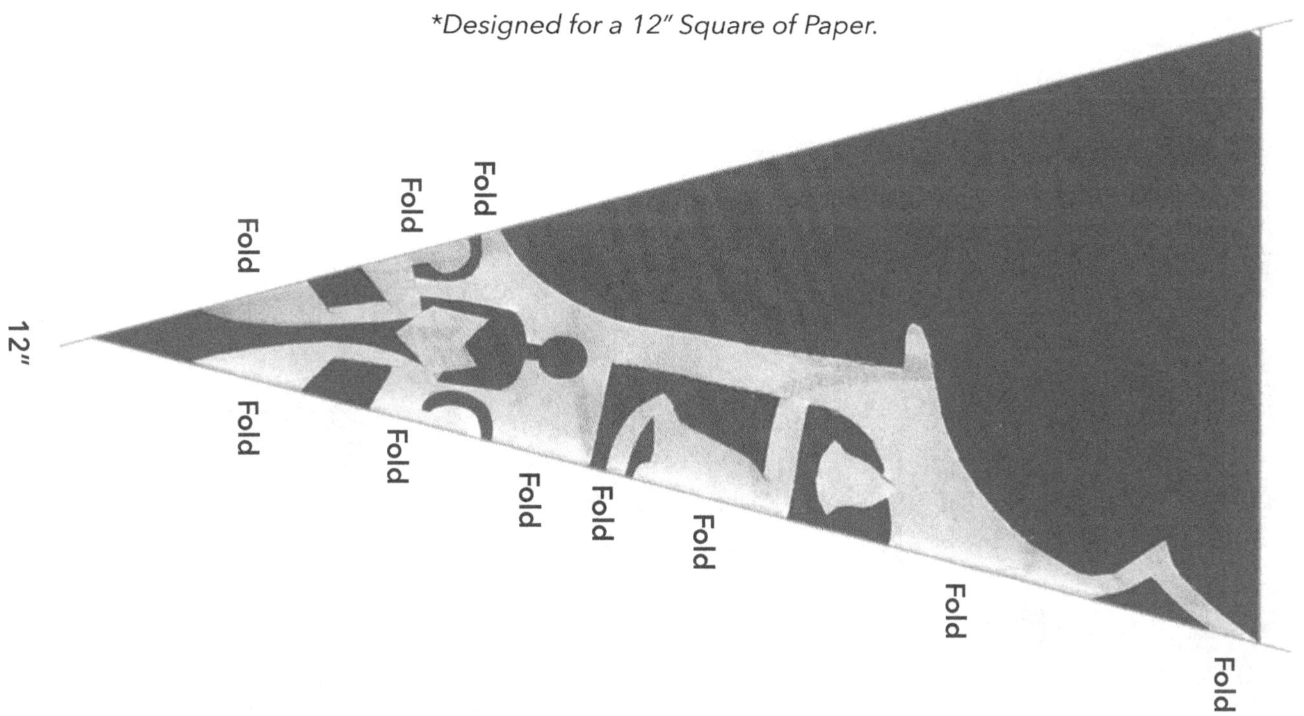

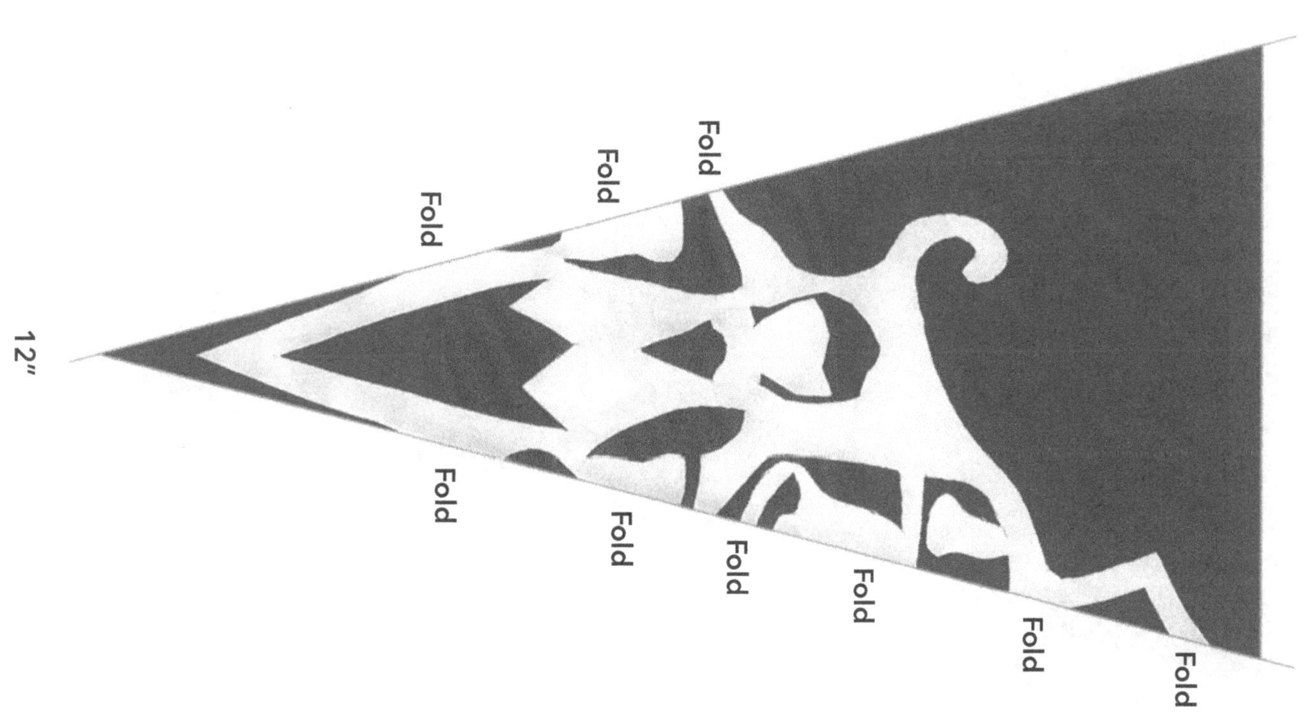

LOVE ONE ANOTHER AND HUMBLE BIRTH

**Designed for a 12" Square of Paper.*

HUMBLE BIRTH 2 AND PRINCE OF PEACE

**Designed for a 12″ Square of Paper.*

PATTERNS

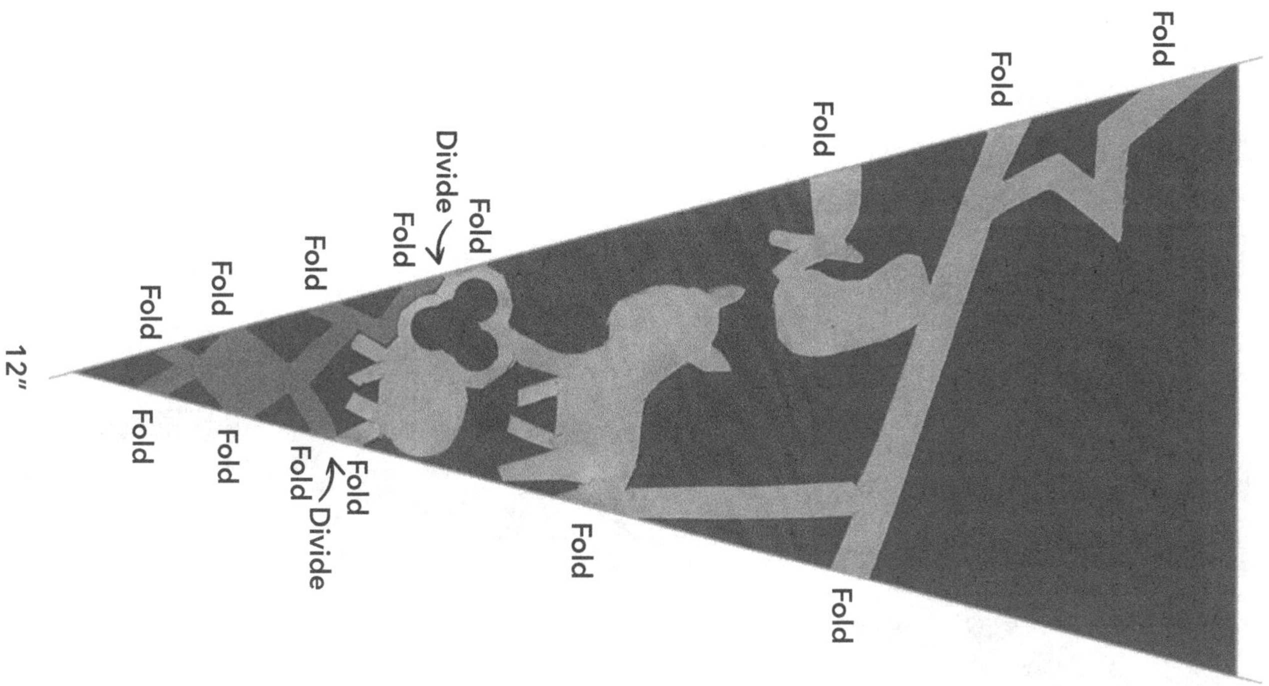

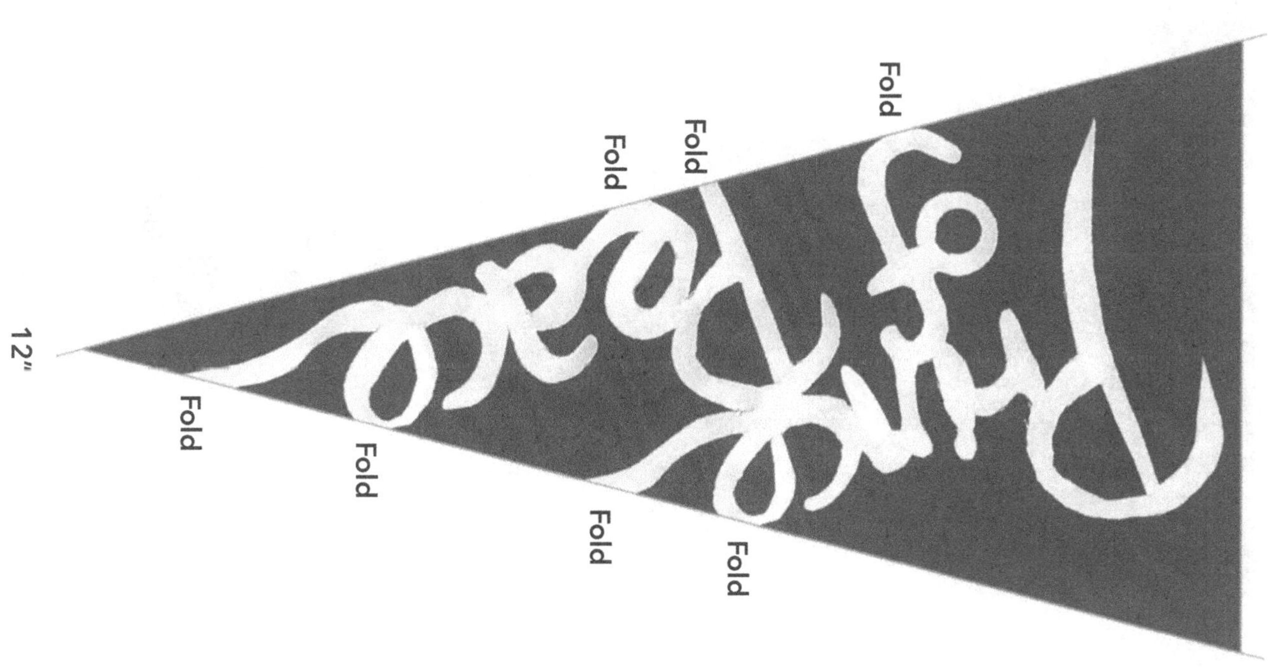

HOPE NATIVITY, DEMO SNOWFLAKE 2, AND JOY TO THE WORLD

**Designed for 12" and 5" Squares of Paper.*

XL NATIVITY

**Designed for a 16″ Square of Paper.*

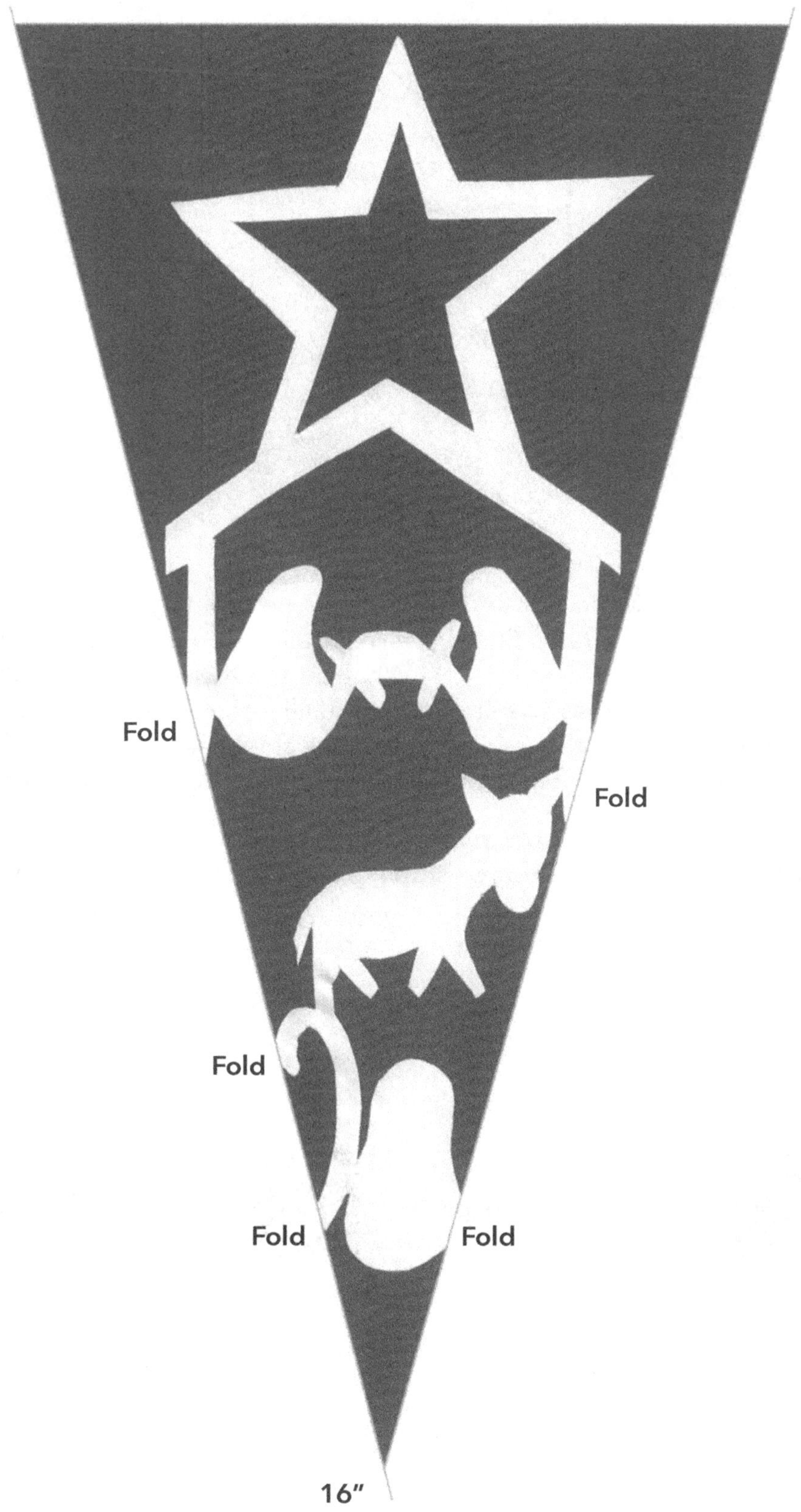

PATTERNS

About the Author

JAMIE GOBLE BROCCO finds it satisfying to take an ordinary piece of paper and turn it into something beautiful! She draws inspiration from scriptures, nature, and Christmas songs to design snowflakes. What began as a relaxing Sabbath Day family activity has evolved as she attempts to fulfill her children's requests and to involve scripture stories in the designs. She uses snowflake patterns to build the readers' abilities, giving them the confidence to create their own designs.

Jamie has learned to find beauty in all seasons! During Iowa winters, she can be found sledding with her children or sipping hot chocolate. In the summer, she enjoys spending time outdoors with her family and harvesting from her edible landscape. There are always memories to be made!

SCAN TO VIEW:
Jamie's Instagram page

SCAN TO VIEW:
Jamie's Pinterest page